SOUTH CENTRAL PENNSYLVANIA LEGENDS AND LORE

SOUTH CENTRAL PENNSYLVANIA LEGENDS AND LORE

DAVID J. PUGLIA

THE
History
PRESS

Published by The History Press
Charleston, SC 29403
www.historypress.net

Copyright © 2012 by David J. Puglia
All rights reserved

Cover images: back, inset: Pennsylvania Dutch fraktur folk art. *Courtesy of the Library of Congress*;
front, bottom: "An Attempt to Burn John Harris at the Present Site of Harrisburg in the
Year 1720" by Ralph Trembly. *Courtesy of the Historical Society of Dauphin County.*

First published 2012

Manufactured in the United States

ISBN 978.1.60949.453.7

Library of Congress CIP data applied for.

For my grandparents,
Robert and Rose Marie Jimeson and Carmen and Tina Puglia.

CONTENTS

ACKNOWLEDGEMENTS

I'm fortunate to have a long list of friends and colleagues I need to thank for helping me write this book. Two men need to be acknowledged first: Simon Bronner and Mac Barrick. Without their dedication to teaching and collecting folklore in South Central Pennsylvania over the past four decades, I would not have had the materials I needed to write a book about the region's folklore. Simon Bronner supported and advised me since our first conversation about the project at the twenty-ninth annual meeting of the International Society for Contemporary Legend Research in Harrisburg. Shippensburg University Spanish professor and Pennsylvania folklorist extraordinaire Mac Barrick died while I was still in elementary school, but working in his collection this past year, I feel as if I've gotten to know him.

The current hosts of the Archives for Pennsylvania Folklife and Ethnography, Heidi Abbey and Penn State Harrisburg's Special Collections, have been supportive and helpful throughout the project. My friends and colleagues Jared Rife, Brant Ellsworth and Spencer Green, as well as their wives Rachel, Coralee and Heather, provided much-needed diversions during the long writing process. Ann and Nancy Swartz and Mira Johnson were the best Dauphin County informants a folklorist could ask for. Michael Barton was the first to bring the legend of "John Harris and the Mulberry Tree" to my attention, and he subsequently guided me to several others. Ken Frew and Stephen Bachmann of the

Historical Society of Dauphin County assisted me in finding some of the vintage images featured in the book and gave me a private tour of the John Harris–Simon Cameron Mansion so I could look at the Philip Harris letter. Charlotte Albert had researched Rehmeyer's Hollow previously and allowed me to benefit from her personal relationship with the Rehmeyer clan. Jim McMahon first told me about Milton Hersey and the *Titanic* and provided me with his research materials.

My parents didn't tell me any legends, but in the dog days of writing, my father mowed my lawn and my mother tidied my house. My commissioning editor, Hannah Cassilly, has been supportive of the project since even before I knew about it. And perhaps most of all, I thank the generations upon generations of folklore students who mined their South Central Pennsylvania hometowns for legends and lore. This book couldn't have been written without them.

INTRODUCTION

Awitch in Williamstown, a glowing fish in Middletown and a hermit in Hummelstown. This is not the history of South Central Pennsylvania; these are its legends and its lore. I cannot promise that everything found in this book is true. Much of it may not be. But I can promise that every story in this volume is authentic folklore, found at one time in the oral tradition of South Central Pennsylvania and presented here with minimal literary embellishment.

This volume presents a wide variety of legends. Some are humorous and others are deadly serious. Throughout the book, I touch on ethnic customs, material culture, religious customs, holiday traditions, songs, dialect jokes, folk heroes, folk villains, ghosts, religious tales, legends of saviors and murderers, legends that are hundreds of years old, legends that are just emerging today, Civil War legends, UFOs, haunted houses, haunted mountains, tales of lovers and much more.

The focus of the text is on South Central Pennsylvania. The action ranges from Berks County in the east to Blair County and Bedford County in the west and up to Centre County in the north, but most legends are set in the strongholds of South Central Pennsylvania: Dauphin County, Lebanon County, Lancaster County, York County, Adams County, Cumberland County, Franklin County, Perry County, Huntingdon County, Mifflin County, Juniata County, Snyder County, Northumberland County and Schuylkill County.

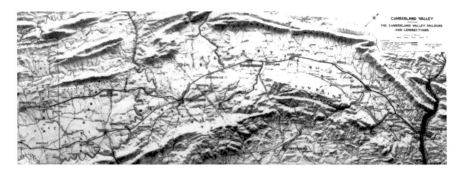

A vintage map of South Central Pennsylvania modeled by Victor Mindeleff in 1912.
Courtesy of the Historical Society of Dauphin County.

The first part covers the legends and customs of the Pennsylvania Dutch, those German immigrants who have made Pennsylvania home for hundreds of years. The second part introduces the reader to some of the folk heroes (and one folk villain) of South Central Pennsylvania. The third part concerns the subject of murderous men. At least one person is accused of murder in every section of the book (a common theme in legends), but in these stories, the killer is the linchpin of the tale. The fourth part of the book focuses on ghosts across the region whose spirits remain in their haunts, usually for one good reason or another. The fifth part of the book is about specific places. A large number of these legends are also supernatural, but I differentiate these legends from the fourth section because they focus primarily on place and secondarily on the supernatural. Others, like the tales of the Chesapeake Nail Works and Three Mile Island, are legendary without being supernatural at all.

Part I

LORE OF THE PENNSYLVANIA DUTCH

HEX SIGNS

A recognizable symbol of the Pennsylvania Dutch, the colorful, multipoint star within a circle decorates barns throughout South Central Pennsylvania, especially in Berks County. Hex signs mystify the general public, which has created its own folklore attempting to explain them. A long debate raged throughout the twentieth century over whether or not hex signs had magical properties and how they connected with Pennsylvania Dutch superstitions. Although the Pennsylvania Dutch have a number of unique folk beliefs, hex signs are not one of them. Alfred Shoemaker—the first state folklorist of Pennsylvania—wrote a pamphlet (*Hex No!*) vigorously emphasizing this.

The Pennsylvania Dutch beautified their property—all of their property. Utensils, furniture and, yes, even barns were all enthusiastically decorated by the Pennsylvania Dutch. The barn was of upmost importance to Pennsylvania Dutch life. This is why they built such immaculate barns and why they decorated them so elaborately. Hex signs are a uniquely American art form, dating back to at least the eighteenth century in Berks County. Although there are no hex signs in Germany, they do have European antecedents. Hex signs are reminiscent of symbols found throughout history, often associated with

Two green, white and red hex signs on a stone-end bank barn on State Route 73 in Colebrookdale Township. *Courtesy of the Library of Congress.*

Three blue, yellow and white compass-pattern hex signs on a stone-end bank barn on State Route 135 in Moselem Springs. *Courtesy of the Library of Congress.*

nature, landowner rights and the sun. The Rosy Cross—the symbol of the German Rosicrucian Order—and hex signs share a remarkable resemblance. In the late twentieth century, two types of hex signs appeared in Pennsylvania—those painted directly onto the sides of barns and those painted on a circle of plywood or masonite. The latter often included distelfinks, hearts, tulips and other gaudy designs.

The first of this type was made in 1950 at the Kutztown Folk Festival. Milton Hill, a hex sign painter from Berks County, was painting four-foot hex signs on large wall sections set up for his demonstration. Visitors wished that they could take the results of the demonstration home. The director of the festival, Alfred Shoemaker, told carpenters to cut out the hex signs and send them home with the festivalgoers. Realizing that there was significant interest in hex signs outside the small circle of Berks County farmers, Milton Hill began painting his hex signs onto wood circles and selling them to tourists. Mysterious Pennsylvania Dutch folk artist Johnny Ott intentionally linked hex signs with magical powers after discovering that it increased his sales. In addition to more traditional designs, he incorporated distelfinks, hearts, doves, tulips and other symbols of the Pennsylvania Dutch. Today, there are a number of contemporary artists working in the genre, a thriving, indigenous American folk art.

OLD-TIME HOME SUPERSTITIONS OF THE PENNSYLVANIA DUTCH

Pennsylvania is known for its almanacs, and the Pennsylvania Dutch believed in following them carefully. Julius Sachse wrote this brief article on the "Prognostics and Superstitions" of the Pennsylvania Dutch in 1907, and it was reprinted in the Pennsylvania-German *in 1907.*

The superstitions of the early German settlers entered into all domestic actions and the duties of every-day life. No matter whether it was the sowing of seed, the reaping of the grain, starting upon a journey, the curing of any disorder in man or beast, the birth or baptism of a child, a marriage or a funeral—in each and every phase of common life there was interspersed more or less of this *Aberglaube*. This was especially true of the settlers of Germantown and the Conestoga country, who were imbued with the notions of mystical religion, and with the speculations of Jacob Boehme and others.

Perhaps the most common of these superstitions was what was known as *Kalender-Aberglaube*, a belief in prognostics based upon the phases of the moon and other celestial bodies, not, however, to be confounded with the custom of astrology or the casting of the horoscope. To any person schooled in the art, the almanac became the guide and mentor for almost every function of daily life. First, it told us of the state of the weather for every day of the coming year; then it informed us what were to be the prevalent diseases, gave us the proper days for felling timber, taking purgative medicine, for bleeding and blood-letting, for cutting the hair, for weaning calves, children, etc. It gave the lucky days for sowing grain, the proper days for a merchant to speculate, and for other daily avocations.

A well regulated German almanac of that day also contained a list of lucky and unlucky days in general, from which we learn that the latter were as follows:

January 1, 2, 6, 11, 17, 19.
February 10, 16, 17.
March 1, 2, 12, 15.
April 3, 15, 17, 18.
May 8, 10, 17, 30.
June 1, 7.
July 1, 5, 6.
August 1, 3, 10, 20.
September 15, 19, 30.
October 15, 1,7.
November 1, 7.
December 1, 7.

There were two days among the list which were far worse than the others, viz.: April 1, the day upon which Satan was expelled from Heaven, and December 1, that day upon which Sodom and Gomorrah was destroyed. It was firmly believed that anyone who had a vein open upon one of those days would surely die within a week. A child born upon either of the two days was sure to die an evil death, would never be old, and would live a life of shame in the world.

Phlebotomy, or bloodletting, was a species of treatment applied at that period to almost every ailment the human race is heir to. No matter whether the patient suffered from a brain fever, dropsy, or simple indigestion—if the signs were right the barber surgeon was at once directed to take so much blood from the sufferer. It was also the custom to be bled in the spring and fall, so as to be kept well during the rest of the year, a custom akin to the one prevalent in the days of our youth, of being drenched with a "yarb tea," a villainous decoction in which hoarhound, gentian and other bitter herbs predominated. According to the well regulated almanac, there were for phlebotomy fourteen bad days in every month. Then we have one day designated as "good," another as the "very best," one "dangerous," one "good in every case," and finally one "very questionable." To illustrate how the days were rated for this purpose we will but mention the following:

> *1. Bad, one loses his color.*
> *2. Bad, causes fever.*
> *23. Very good, prevents all sickness and strengthens all the limbs of the body.*

Then we have the various astrological signs of the almanac, which gave the proper days for cutting timber, etc.; also for taking medicines. So strongly was this belief seated in the minds of the populace that cases are known in which sick persons died, inasmuch as they persistently refused to take the remedy prescribed by the doctor until the signs should be right; and the delay proved fatal.

What chemist ever discovered such a cheap and effectual method of putting acetic acid into a barrel of cider as our dear old forefathers in this country less than a hundred years ago? After the cider was put into the cask, it was only necessary to call up the names of three of the crossest, most sour-tempered old women in the community and in a loud tone of voice utter their names into the bung-hole, and immediately cork it up, to make the best and strongest vinegar in all the neighborhood. When now and then some female in the community was inclined to show an unnecessary degree of temper, her friends would jokingly remind her that she might waken up some frosty autumn morning and find herself in a vinegar barrel!

The belief that a savage dog could be charmed out of harm by incantations was everywhere prevalent. All that was required to do this was to repeat certain words or verses, which I no longer remember, before entering upon the dog's premises, and at the same time pull up a fence-stake and reverse its position in the ground. These things done, the dog's mouth was sealed, and the visitor was relived of all danger from the canine's teeth, until the reversed fence-stake was again placed in its natural position.

Another and more pleasant superstition of the early German settlers was their belief in the virtues of the Domestic Benison or *Haus-Segen*, a written or printed invocation prominently displayed on the walls of the living room and, in many cases, recited daily as a morning/evening prayer. This Benison was usually a small printer sheet, frequently ornamented or embellished with allegorical figures, frequently crude pictures representing angels and symbolic flowers.

The best-known and perhaps most widely circulated of these domestic invocations consists of four verses and an invocation:

> *In the three most exalted names,*
> *Father, Son and Holy Ghost,*
> *That are praised by angelic choirs,*
> *Health, Peace and Blessing—Amen.*

The first verse invokes the blessing of God upon the house and ground, the coming harvest and growing crops, that the cattle may increase, and that God, in His fatherly goodness, will protect house, estate, stable and barn from all mishaps, especially fire.

The second verse pleads that the glow of health may shine upon every cheek, prays for strength for our labor, and that neither hail nor storm may injure the tender blossoms, nor late frosts and early colds kill the fruit.

The third verse is a supplication that the blessed Redeemer extend His power and influence over the house and family, that everyone therein may strive after virtue and live peacefully, so that all sin and wickedness be a stranger to this house.

Finally, the prayer asks that the Holy Ghost abide here and take up his resting place; bless our outgoing home-coming, and in the end grant unto us a blessed death and receive us as heirs of heaven.

MAN ON THE MULE

The Man on the Mule in Greencastle is the most famous brick-end barn in the world and has been for some time. An illustration of it graces the cover of Alfred Shoemaker's *The Pennsylvania Barn*, published in 1955. It still stands today. Legend says that a wealthy farmer coveted his prize

The Man on the Mule brick-end barn in Greencastle, Pennsylvania. *Author's private collection.*

horse above all else. Employing a mason to build a brick-end barn, he decreed that the end design would show him on his steed. During construction, an argument arose between the mason and the farmer, and the mason was told that he would not be paid what he had expected. When the farmer took a trip west to see his daughter, he demanded the mason finish the barn before he returned. The chagrined mason swapped out the farmer's stallion and placed him on a jackass instead. A second legend claims that the barn depicts Jesus riding his donkey into Jerusalem on Palm Sunday. The current owner believes the barn was a clandestine place of worship for a religious group active in the area.

AMISH BLUE GATE

The Amish are a well-known religious group found in Southeastern and South Central Pennsylvania. They refer to themselves as "Plain People," a term that contrasts them with the "Gay Dutch" or "Fancy Dutch"—the Pennsylvania German settlers who were not members of the Amish or Mennonite Church. They are committed to simple living, plain clothing and a resistance to unnecessary modern technology. Anyone who has lived in an area with an Amish population will be familiar with the traditional Amish horse-driven buggy used for transportation, as well as the accompanying traffic signs. The Amish came to Pennsylvania at the same time as non-Amish German immigrants, and their material culture is very similar to that of their "Gay" neighbors, but without the decorative adornments.

As they spread across the country to the Midwest and elsewhere, the Amish took elements of South Central Pennsylvania culture with them. The Amish are particularly identifiable by their unique mode of dress. Although this dress seems unusual now, it is really just the general dress of the nineteenth-century American farmer, untouched by modern changes in fashion. One longstanding Pennsylvania legend concerns the Amish blue gate. Put simply, the legend states that when an Amish father's daughter becomes available for marriage, he signals her availability by painting his front gate blue. The strange thing about this legend is that, despite its ubiquity, a drive through Amish country will consistently reveal no blue gates. Are there really that few eligible Amish maidens?

David Luthy attributed the false belief to a number of sources, beginning with Berenice Steinfeldt's 1937 *The Amish of Lancaster County*. Amish Country had become a popular tourist destination, and Steinfeldt wrote her book to cash in on this trend. The cover of the book featured a drawing based on a photograph of two Amish men talking. In the photograph, the men stand in front of a brick wall. In the drawing, the men stand in front of a blue gate. In the pamphlet, Steinfeldt wrote, "The sign of a blue painted gate grew to be the advertising sign of an Amish daughter ready to marry." The popularity, reprinting and wide distribution of the pamphlet encouraged the legend. Although Pennsylvanians seem to like the idea, the Amish simply don't need such visual indicators.

Amish communities are notoriously tightknit. When an Amish girl turns sixteen, she joins an Amish youth group, where she will meet the available Amish boys. Young bachelors know who the eligible ladies

An Amish family getting into their traditional horse-drawn carriage. *Courtesy of the Library of Congress.*

are long before their father has a chance to slap any paint on his front gate. At least one prominent Amish man, Bishop Benjamin F. Beiler, did have a blue gate, but his was for directing visitors, not suitors, to his house. Although the idea of the blue gate seems to have no traditional importance in Amish life, it has taken on a life of its own as an indicator of "Amishness." Places like the Blue Gate Restaurant and the Blue Gate Theater, located in Amish country and targeting tourists, take advantage of the old legend.

BELSNICKEL

Belsnickel is both a noun and a verb. Belsnickel is a Christmastime character found in Pennsylvania Dutch communities, but children can also "belsnickel" on Christmas Eve. The former is described in the Pottstown LaFayette Aurora *on December 21, 1826, in the first column. The latter is described in the second column in the* Reading Weekly Eagle *on December 31, 1892. Although they use the same term, notice the difference in tone between the two articles.*

Bellsnickel. This is a mischievous hobgoblin that makes his presence known to the people once a year by his cunning trick of fairyism. Christmas is the time for his sporting revelry, and he then gives full scope to his permitted privileges in every shape that his roving imagination can suggest. Pottstown has had a full share of his presence this season if I am to judge from the wreck of lumber that is strewed throughout streets and blockading the doors generally every morning, which indicates the work of a mighty marauder. A few mornings since a little before sunrise, as I was wending my way past your office, I beheld a complete bridge built across the street, principally composed of old barrels, hogshead, grocery boxes, wheelbarrows, harrows, plows, wagon and cart wheels. It is reported that he nearly demolished a poor woman's house in one of the back streets a few nights ago. He performs these tricks *incog*, or otherwise he would be arrested long since by the public authorities, who are on the alert; but it will take a swift foot and a strong arm to apprehend him while he is in full power of his bellsnickleship, as he then can evade mortal ken.

He has the appearance of a man of 50, and is about 4 feet high, red round face, curly black hair, with a long beard hanging perpendicular from his chin, and his upper lip finely graced with a pair of horned mustachios, of which a Turk would be proud; he is remarkably thick being made in a puncheon style, and is constantly laughing, which occasions his chunky frame to be in a perpetual shake; he carries a great budget on his back, filled with all the dainties common to the season—he cracks his nuts amongst the people as well as his jokes without their perceiving him.

His antique clothing cannot pass unnoticed, as a description of its comical fashion may excite some ambition amongst the dandies, who are always on the look-out for something flash and neat, beyond what an honest, industrious, plain mechanic wears, to correspondent their mode of dress with his, whose costume is entirely novel to the present generation; besides the French and English fashions are completely exhausted and have become obsolete; therefore, a description of his grotesque raiment I presume will be acceptable.

The genus of the night winds and storms is, when at a distance, entirely a nondescript; but when he approaches his uncouth magnitude diminishes, and you can accurately survey his puncheon frame from top to toe. His cap, a queer one indeed, is made of a black bearskin, fringed round or rather stuck round with porcupine quills painted a fiery red, and having two folds at each side, with which he at pleasure covers his neck and part of his funny face, giving sufficient scope for his keen eye to penetrate on both sides when he is on his exploits of night-errantry.

His outer garment, like Joseph's of old, is of many colors, made in the Adamitish mode, hanging straight down from his shoulders to his heels, with a tightening belt attached to the waist—the buttons seem to be manufactured entirely in an ancient style—out of the shells of hickory nuts, with an eye of whalebone ingeniously fixed in each,—when he runs, the tail of his long coat flies out behind, which gives an opportunity to behold his little short red plush breeches, with brass kneebuckles attached to their extremities, the size of a full moon. His stockings are composed of green buckram, finely polished. His moccasins are the same as those worn by the Chippewa nation. He carries a bow with a sheaf of arrows thrown across his miscellaneous budget, thus equipped, he sallies forth in the dark of night, with a few tinkling bells attached to his bear skin cap and the tail of his long cap, and makes as much noise as mischief through our town, while the peaceable inhabitants are quietly reposing under the influence of Morpheus.

In some parts of Berks, the "belsnickel" parties have ceased making their annual visits, but in most sections they are still keeping up the old custom and having lots of fun, too. In the northern part of the county parties of this kind are especially large.

At six o'clock on Christmas eve unusual bustle broke the customary quiet of the big kitchen of a certain farmhouse near the Blue Mountains. There were fourteen boys, ranging in age from fourteen to twenty years, in the kitchen, and seven or eight more were on the porch outside. The kitchen and porch were noisy with the continuous passing in and out and laughing and rompings of the boys.

On the wood chest, behind the big woodstove in the kitchen, sat a short but very stout man, aged about sixty-five, and by his side sat his wife, a woman of medium weight, but a few years older than her husband. The marks left by years of hard work could be plainly seen on both. The old man couldn't talk for laughing. The old lady, however, was busy chatting with the young people about her. Around a table near the center of the room sat six girls, two of whom are daughters of the house. All the girls were laughing and chatting with boys. Two of the sons went round and spoke hurriedly to the others, giving instructions.

At half past six o'clock the six girls, the two old people and the two sons went into an adjoining room, where there was a big head of old clothes, including Shaker bonnets, which were worn so extensively by women forty years ago, hoop skirts, Piccadilly collars, linen dusters, high silk hats of ancient fashion, etc.

On one of the window sills there were a lot of masks, such as are sold in the Reading variety stores. Soon four of the boys in the kitchen were also called into the side room, where each of them was turned into a Santa Claus, or belsnickel. The girls dressed two of the boys in women's clothes, as grotesquely as possible. The two brothers helped the two others dress ludicrously in men's clothes. Next the face of each boy was blacked with burned cork, so that nobody could discover their identity in case the masks should give away, as sometimes happens.

In this way fourteen young people were rigged up as full fledged belsnickels. The old people and the girls laughed heartily. The two brothers were the last to assume disguise. Shortly before eight o'clock the party was ready to start out. Some had peanuts, some candy, others dried apples or pears, others nuts, and still others popcorn. Before they left the old lady gave them a bag containing about a peck of dried pears. When outside the house each took a hickory "gad" they had brought along from home with the rest of their paraphernalia the evening before.

When the party had gone and the girls were in another room the old man, who had but a short time before laughed so heartily, said, with tears in his eyes: "This makes me think of the time when I was young. How we used to have fun on Christmas eve. That time we had larger parties than the one that just left. Those dear old times are right before me tonight. I haven't been so happy in a year as now, but still, when I think of the fact that all those who used to travel with me from farm house to farm house the night before Christmas are now dead, I cannot keep back the tears. These boys that just left our house have brought back to me memories that couldn't be awakened in any other way. I can't see why some people are so foolish nowadays as to not to allow their children to "act belsnickel." It makes me happy to see them happy."

The Santa Claus party that left this farmer's house, visited farm house after farm house. They gave the children chestnuts, popcorn, dried apples, candy, etc., and the obstreperous ones they whipped a little. Many of the farmers gave the party apples and cider. At about midnight they ate a hearty dinner at a farmhouse about four miles from the place from which they started. They said they would make a trip of about ten miles, and arrive home about six o'clock the next morning. The average party wasn't as large as this one and didn't make as large a trip.

Pork and Sauerkraut on New Year's Day

The lines between regional and ethnic culture can sometimes be blurry, as seen in New Year customs. South Central Pennsylvania families have passed down the regional tradition of pork and sauerkraut on the New Year from generation to generation. The belief in eating pork and sauerkraut in Pennsylvania is based on the folk concept of "like produces like." By eating items associated with growth and prosperity (especially in German tradition)—the pig is an animal whose weight can increase quickly, and the cabbage is a plant that can spread remarkably—Pennsylvanians want to produce a similar result of growth in the coming year. A comparable idea but in a different form is found in Hoppin' John, a dish made from black-eyed peas and rice, often with a pork product. The traditional roots there are thought to come from African traditions. Rice, a food that expands, can be found in the special making of "mochi" rice cakes among Japanese Americans, often in different colors. They are sweetened, which means that they ensure not only a year of growth but of sweetness, an idea also evident in the consumption of apples and honey for the Jewish New Year.

The Ballad of Susanna Cox

In 1809, young German immigrant Susanna Cox found herself with child. Unmarried and uneducated, she killed her infant rather than admit to having a child out of wedlock (the father was her married neighbor). Caught and accused of infanticide, she spoke little English and was unable to defend herself in court. She was quickly tried and hanged in Reading, but many were sympathetic to her plight. A ballad written about her, first in German and then in English, became incredibly popular. A dramatic reenactment takes place daily at the annual Kutztown Folk Festival. A reading of the poem from the gallows precedes the hanging of a Susanna Cox effigy.

Lore of the Pennsylvania Dutch

A New Dirge,
containing
The History of Susanna Cox
who was executed at Reading for the murder of her own child.

"The story I'm going to tell you,
Forever will be new,
And who but once doth hear it,
'T will break his heart in two."

All ye who feel for others' woes,
With hearts compassionate,
Oh!! listen to the woeful tale,
Of a poor damsel's fate!

Susanna Cox, a country-maid,
Young, and of beauty rare,
In Oley as a servant had
Long lived with Jacob Gehr.

Ne'er had she been instructed in
The course of human law,
Nor did she know God's Holy Word,
Which strikes the world with awe.

For, ev'ry one must be aware
Of what he daily sees,
That who the scriptures don't restrain,
They'll do just what they please.

Her neighbor, well remember we—
Merz was his second name—
He recklessly led her astray
By lust's unhallowed flame.

An instance which, from Adam's time,
The race of man defiled,
When Satan, in a serpent's garb,
His help-mate Eve beguiled.

Death followed in seduction's train,
When the first the world began—
This happened to Susanna Cox
Through that unworthy man.

What is his seventh commandment God,
What sacred laws forbid,
He wantonly trod under foot
And laughed, and scoffed at it.

Though married, to seduce this girl
He did not hesitate—
He'll rue it when he's dead and gone,
But then 'twill be too late!

Fear of disgrace prevented her
From making known her state,
Which she by ev'ry means concealed
Despair did indicate.

The eighteen hundred and ninth year,
At half past four at morn,
The fourteenth day of February,
The unhappy child was born.

So far misled this sinner was,
So much bewildered she,
That she her helpless infant's soul
Sent to eternity.

As soon as rumor did at her
Point as a murderess,
Off was she hurried to the jail,
The foul deed to confess.

A jury then empannelled was
To investigate her case,
And to decide accordingly
What sentence should take place.

Although she supplicated hard
To pardon her great sin,
Of murder in the first degree
They guilty brought her in.

Ere long she in the court-house was
Arraigned before Judge Spayd,
Where, shedding many scorching tears,
She learned her awful fate.

Each one may easily conceive
What her own feelings were
To think, Oh lamentable case!
What end awaited her.

Then to the Governor was sent,
Who lived in Lancaster,
The warrant which contained her doom,
For his own signature.

A gentleman who pitied her,
Had by himself been sent
To supplicate the Executive
Law's rigor to suspend.

A woman reads the ballad of Susanna Cox before the dramatic reenactment of the hanging at the annual Kutztown Folk Festival. *Author's private collection.*

But she no pardon could obtain,
For she was to be hung
As early as the tenth of June,
To war both old and young.

The warrant was returned, and read
In her dark prison-cell,
When fervently she prayed to God
To save her soul from hell.

The clergy oft did visit her
In her repentant state,
For earnestly she penance did,
Preparing for her fate.

Lore of the Pennsylvania Dutch

Just as the clock did strike elev'n,
She straightways from the jail
Was led to where the gallows stood,
Oh lamentable tale!

She faithfully admonished all,
Young folks especially,
"Oh let," said she, "my dreadful fate
To you a warning be."

She humbly knelt upon the ground,
And called in her distress
Upon the Lord to pardon all
Her sins and wickedness.

So piteous her crying was,
Her anguish and her fears so great
That ev'ry heart was moved,
And ev'ry eye shed tears.

She said: "I in an instant shall
Go to eternity;
Oh God! for my redeemer's sake,
Turn not they face from me!"

She then was made to undergo
The punishment of death;
Scarce sev'nteen minutes had expired
When she resigned her breath.

Although without the least delay
Their skill the doctors tried,
To bring her back to life against
Was to their art denied.

He that composed this little song,
In mem'ry of the event,
Was present at the closing scene,
And did the trial attend.

Let all who live upon this earth,
By her example see,
What dire disgrace may those befall
Who're raised illiterately.

Short was, and sad, her pilgrimage,
Her youth mere drudgery,
Her age but twenty years and four,
Her exit—infamy.

Pennsylvania Dutch Dialect Jokes

The Pennsylvania Dutch speak in a noticeable accent that has amused their neighbors for generations. So amusing was the accent that an imitation of the dialect alone could form the foundation of a joke. The humor in the following three texts is based on just that gag. The first is a legend told about a Pennsylvania Dutchman in which his and his family's dialogue abound. Davy Crockett tells the second while electioneering in Tennessee. The third is a humorous Christmas poem in exaggerated Pennsylvania Dutch dialect.

The Snake Bitten Dutchman

Some years ago, near the town of Reading, Berks County, Pennsylvania, there lived a cozy old farmer named Sweighoffer—of German descent, and accent too, as his speech will indicate. Old man Sweighoffer had once served as a member in the legislature and was therefore "no fool"; and as he had also long commanded a volunteer corps of rustic militia, he should hardly be supposed to incline to cowardice. His son, Peter, was his only son, a strapping lad of seventeen; and upon old Peter and young Peter devolved the principal cares and toils of the old gentleman's farm, now and then assisted by the old lady and her two bouncing daughters—for it is very common in that State to see the women and girls at work in the fields—and on extra occasions by some hired hands. Well, one warm day in haying time, old Peter and young Peter were hard at it in the meadow when the old man drops his scythe and bawls out, "O, mine Gott, Peter!"

"What's de matter, fader!" answered the son, straightening up and looking at his sire.

"Oh, mine Gott, Peter!" again cried the old fellow.

"Donder," echoed young Peter, hurrying up to the old man.

"O mine Gott, der shnake bite mine leg!"

If any thing in particular was capable of frightening young Peter, it was snakes—for he had once nearly crippled himself for life by trampling on a crooked stick, which cramped his ankle and so horrified the young man that he liked to have fallen through himself. At the word "snake," young Peter fell back, nimbly as a wire-drawer, and bawled out in turn, "Where is der shnake?"

"Up my trowsis, Peter-O, mine Gott!"

"O mine Gott!" echoed Peter, junior, "kill him, fader, kill him."

"No-a, no-a, he kill me, Peter; come—come quick—get it off my trowsis!" But Peter the younger's cowardice overcame his filial affection, while his fear lent strength to his legs, and he started like a scared locomotive to call the old burly (Pennsylvania) Dutchman, who was in a distant part of the field, to give his father a lift with the snake.

Old Jake, the farmer's assistant, came bounding along as soon as he heard the news, passing along the fence whereon Peter and his boy had hung their "linsey-woolsey" vests. Jake grabbed one of the garments and hurried to the old man Peter, who still managed to keep on his pins, although he was quaking and trembling like an aspen leaf in a jungle gale of wind.

"O, mine Gott! Come, come quick, Yacob. He bite me all to pieces—here up mine leg."

Old Jake was not particularly sensitive to fear, but few people, young or old, are dead to alarm when a "pizenous" reptile is about. Gathering up the stiff dry stalks of a stalwart weed, old Jake told the boss to stand steady, and he would at least stun the snake by a rap or two, if he did not kill her stone dead; the old man Peter, less loth to have legs broken than to be bitten to death by a snake, designated the spot to strike, and old Jake let him have it. The first blow broke the weed and knocked old Sweighoffer off his pegs and into a hay-cock—cobim.

"Oh!" roared old Peter, "you broke mine leg and de shnake's gone!"

"Vere? Vere?" cried old Jake, moving briskly about and scanning very narrowly the ground he stood on.

"Never mind him, Yacob; help me up. I'll go home."

"Put on your vhest, den; here it is;" said the old crout-eater, gathering up his boss and trying to get the garment on his lumpy back. The moment old Peter made this effort, he grew livid in the face; his hair stood on end, "like the quills upon the frightful porcupine," as Mrs. Partington observed—he shivered—he shook—his teeth chattered—and his knees knocked a staccato accompaniment.

"Oh, Yacob, carry me home! I'm dead as nits!"

"Vat! Ish nodder shnake in your troushers?"

"No-a—look, I'm swelt all up! Mine vhest won't go on my back. O, O, mine Gott!"

"Dunder and blixen!" cried old Jake, as he took the same conclusion, and with might and main the old man, scared into a most wonderful feat of physical activity and strength, lugged and carried the boss some quarter of a half a mile to the house.

Young Peter had shinned it home at the earliest stage of the dire proceedings and so alarmed the girls that they were in high state when they saw the approach of the good old dad and his assistant.

Old man Peter was carried in and began to die as natural as life when in comes the old lady, in a great bustle, and wanted to know what was going on. Old Peter, in the last gasp of agony and weakness, opened his eyes and feebly pointed to his leg. The old woman ripped up the pantaloons, and out fell a small thistle top, and at the same time considerable of a scratch was made visible.

"Call dis a shnake! Bah!" says the old woman.

"O, but I'm pizhen—mine vhest—O dear, mine vhest not come over mine body!"

"Haw haw haw!" roared the old woman. "Vat a fool! You got Peter's vhest on—haw, haw, haw!"

"Bosh!" roars old Peter, shaking of death's icy fetters at one surge, and jumping up. "Bosh, Yacob, vat an old fool you musht be, to say I vash schnakebite? Go 'bout your bishness, gals. Peter, bring me some beer."

The old woman saved Peter's life.

Davy Crockett and the Tam Harricoon

While electioneering, the colonel [Davy Crockett] always conciliates every crowd into which he may be thrown by the narration of some anecdote. It is his *manner*, more than the anecdote, which delights you. Having been a great deal with the [Pennsylvania] Dutch, he draws very liberally on them whenever he wants to make sport. I once had the pleasure of seeing Colonel Crockett the centre of some dozen persons, to whom he was telling the following story of a [Pennsylvania] Dutchman, thus went on:

Well, tam it, what you tink, a tam harricoon come to my hinkle stall [hen-house] *an picked out ebery hair out de backs of all my young hinkles; so I goes ober to brudder Richards, and gets his fox trap; an as I comes back, I says to myself, I'll catch de tam harricoon. So I takes de fox trap an goes to my hinkle stall, an I didn't set it outside, and I didn't set it inside, but I puts it down jist dere. So next morning I goes to my hinkle stall, an sure enough I had de tam harricoon fast; an he wasn't white, and he wasn't black, an ebery hair was off he tail* [opossum], *an soon as he see me, he look so shame—ah! you tam harricoon, you kill my hinkles, heh! an I hit him a lick, an he lay down, an he look so sorry, he make me tink he repent; so I turn him loose. Well, now what do you tink; I goes to my hinkle stall next morning, and dere lay my old speckled hinkle, an ebery hair was out her back; so I goes ober to brudder Richard's gin, an gits his fox trap, to catch de tam harricoon; an I carried it to de hinkle stall, an I didn't set it outside, an I didn't set it inside, but I puts it jist dere; an sure enough, next morning I had de old haricoon gin; an he wasn't white, and he wasn't black; but he was white, an he was black, spotted all ober* [pole cat], *an I goes up*

to him, ah! yo's de tam harricoon dat catch my old speckled hinkle, heh!
you de tam rascal! an I hits him a lick, and he lif he tail up, an don't
you tink I smelt him?

Dot Leedle Fur Cap

Der next night vas Christmas, der night it vas shtill,
Der stockings ver hung by der chimney to fill.

Nuddings vas shtirring at all in der house,
For fear dot St. Nicholas vas nicht comen herause.

Der children were dried und gone to der bed,
Und Mudder in her nightgown and I on ahead.

Vas searching avround in the closets for toys,
Ve krept around kviet, not to raise any noise.

Now Mudder vas carrying all the toys in her gown,
Showing her person, from up her vaist down.

Den as ve come near de crib of our boy,
Our youngest and sveetest, our pride and our choy.

His eyes opened wide as he peeked from his cot,
Und seen efreytink dot his mutter has got.

But he didn't efen notice der toys in her lap,
He chust asked "For who is dot leedle fur cap?"

Un Mutter said "hush" und she laff vit delight,
"I think I giff dat to your fodder tonight."

Part II
FOLK HEROES AND LEGENDS

DIRK WILLEMS

Dirk Willems is our only folk hero who is not a Pennsylvanian. In fact, he lived and died long before William Penn ever set food in his woods. Regardless, Dirk Willems is an important folk hero in Pennsylvania, especially among the Amish. Although he is known in oral tradition as well, his story was captured in print hundreds of years ago in the Martyrs Mirror. *This is the best-known version of the legend.*

This year, Dirk Willems, a faithful brother, and a follower of Jesus Christ, was imprisoned at Asperen, in Holland, and had to suffer evil tyranny from the Roman Catholics. But as he had not built his faith and confidence on the movable sand of human commandments; but on the first foundation stone, Christ Jesus, he remained steadfast and immovable unto the end, not withstanding the tempests of human doctrine, and the floods of tyrannical and cruel persecution. Hence, when the Supreme Shepherd shall appear in the clouds of heaven, to gather together his elect from the ends of the earth, he also shall hear: Well done good and faithful servant, thou hast been faithful over a few things, I will make thee ruler over many things, enter thou into the joy of thy Lord.

The following authentic account is given of his apprehension: He had escaped and fled, and was closely pursued by a jailor, but as there

Hearing the crack of the ice when escape was all but certain, Dirk Willems turned around and pulled his pursuer from the icy waters. *From* The Bloody Theater; or, Martyrs Mirror.

was ice on the water, Dirk Willems got over with some danger, but the jailor who was in pursuit, broke through and fell in; observing that he was in danger of his life, Willems ran immediately to the jailor's assistance, and helped him out, and saved his life. The jailor wanted to let him go, but the burgomaster called sharply to him, that he should consider his oath; thus he was re-taken by the jailor, and after steadfastly enduring a severe imprisonment, and great opposition from these blood-thirsty and ravenous wolves; he was burnt to death over a slow fire, and sealed with his blood and death, the pure faith, and the unadulterated truth, for an example of instruction, to all pious Christians of the present time, and to the everlasting disgrace of the tyrannical papists.

ANN, THE WITCH OF WILLIAMSTOWN

About seventy years ago, an elderly woman named Ann lived in Williamstown. Everyone who knew Ann believed she was a witch who cast evil spells on her neighbors. One day, walking down the street past her neighbor Debbie's house, she paused to admire the Blue Flag flowers sitting on Debbie's front porch. Ann asked Debbie if she could have a slip of the plant for her own yard. Debbie feared giving Ann *anything*, so she made an excuse and promised to bring her a Blue Flag some other time. A few days later, Debbie took a walk to visit her mother. Traversing an alley, she stumbled upon Ann once again. Ann put her hand on Debbie's shoulder and reminded her to pick up the baby powder at her house. When Ann touched her shoulder, Debbie felt an electric shock course through her body. Debbie had left the baby powder a few days ago at a relative's house, and through a series of events, it somehow had made its way to Ann's house. Debbie walked to Ann's house to get the baby powder, and there she noticed Blue Flags already growing in Ann's garden. Convinced that Ann was looking for a way to hex her, Debbie retrieved the baby powder without incident, but as soon as she made it home, she tossed the bottle directly into the furnace.

Another time, Ann asked another a neighbor to pick cherries "for the half" (half for her and half for him). After the neighbor picked the cherries, he gave half to Ann and half to his wife. His wife jarred their share, but when it came time for them to eat their cherries, every single jar had spoiled. The couple was sure that Ann had hexed their half of the cherries.

On yet another day, Ann journeyed half a mile to another neighbor's house to ask for a bit of salt. The neighbor granted the request, and Ann turned around and walked back home. Later that night, the good wife told her husband that she had let Ann borrow some salt earlier that day. Her husband immediately stood up, grabbed the salt and tossed what was left straight into the furnace.

Yet another neighbor accused Ann of hexing her husband, this time fatally. At midnight on the night of her husband's death, his wife said that all of her clocks stopped ticking and her house fell deathly silent. She could feel that Ann had hexed her husband at that moment and that it ultimately caused his death.

Although Williamstown is full of stories about Ann's hexes, there was at least one sure-fire protection against them. Debbie remembered that while passing Ann's house, she had to chant "kiss my ass" three times in row. Chanted correctly, Ann's hexes could do no harm.

MILTON HERSHEY AND THE *TITANIC*

On April 15, 1912, the sinking of the *Titanic* claimed 1,502 lives, more than two-thirds of the passengers on board. If not for a last-minute change in plans, chocolate pioneer, philanthropist and local hero Milton Hershey would have been one of them. On December 18, 1911, about four months before the *Titanic* set sail, Mr. Hershey deposited $300 to reserve a spot for his wife and him on the state-of-the-art passenger liner. Hershey was heading back to the United States from a trip to Europe, and the new RMS *Titanic* was all the rage. In a lucky twist of fate for Mr. Hershey, he canceled his *Titanic* reservations and instead chose to sail on the German cruise ship *Amerika*, which would put him in New York a few days earlier. Even stranger, the *Titanic* received a warning from a ship ahead of it to be on the lookout for massive icebergs. The ship that sent the warning? The *Amerika*.

The day before the collision, Captain Knuth sent a message to the Hydrographic Office in Washington, D.C., warning of two large icebergs. The message was actually sent through the *Titanic* because the *Amerika* did not have enough radio power. The *Titanic* radio operator then passed the message on. He did not, however, inform his own ship's command, despite the *Titanic* heading for the coordinates given by the *Amerika*. Separating this legend from many like it, there exists physical proof of its veracity. The Hershey Community Archives holds the check made out to White Star Line by Mr. Hershey for the reservation. Choosing to stay in Europe rather than catch the *Amerika* back to the United States, Mrs. Hershey penned a note to her mother on the back of a German postcard: "For Mother—This is an old castle & see how they wall up the sides of mountain grow grapes up on side of very steep grade. Just heard of sinking of the big steamer. How thankful I am God directs to safety in our travels. We are having cold crisp weather here. Hope for warmer soon. Love from Kitty."

The town of Hershey would be a different place if Hershey had perished on the *Titanic*. Mr. Hershey had already established his well-known Hershey Chocolate Company and the Milton Hershey School, but the town of Hershey was still a work in progress. Mr. Hershey had not yet established the now-defunct Hershey Junior College, nor had he created the Derry Township Public School Trust, which lessens the tax burden on Derry Township residents. He hadn't built the Parkview golf course yet nor the Spring Creek golf course. The Hershey Country Club was still years away. There would have been no Hershey Stadium and no Hershey Bears. He had yet to build the Hershey Museum, the Hershey Theater or the Hershey Gardens. And there would have been no Community Building and Theatre and no Hotel Hershey.

THE HUMMELSTOWN HERMIT

William Wilson was born in the eighteenth century but became legendary for his actions in the nineteenth century. He was born in South Central Pennsylvania but spent his formative years in Chester County. Both he and his sister, Elizabeth, were sent away as teenagers—some say because of an "evil stepmother." William returned to South Central Pennsylvania, apprenticing as a stone carver. Elizabeth, on the other hand, took a job as a tavern wench in Philadelphia. At the Indian Queen Tavern, Elizabeth got too close with one of the regulars and soon became plump with child.

Having a pregnant woman on the premises was not considered proper at the time, so Elizabeth was sent away. The "regular" soon became absent, and Elizabeth was forced to fend for herself. She returned to her family in Chester County, where she gave birth to twins. Although Elizabeth's lover had disappeared, she maintained a secret correspondence with him. In October 1784, Elizabeth snuck out to meet him, disappearing for several days. No one knows for certain what happened over these few days, but it would set off a chain of events that would change Elizabeth and William's lives forever. When Elizabeth returned after several days' absence, her twins were not with her. When the twins' corpses were found concealed in the woods, Elizabeth was arrested and charged with murder. Within a year, she had been convicted of murdering her sons and sentenced to hang.

Although initially unaware of his sister's alleged crime and subsequent conviction, William was able to see his sister before she was executed. Elizabeth professed her innocence to William, claiming that it was her former lover who had murdered her children. After killing her children, he threatened to do the same to her if she ever said a word to anyone. William convinced Elizabeth to maintain her silence no longer. For the first time, Elizabeth revealed the truth to local officials. Her confession went before the Supreme Executive Council. The council ordered a reprieve until January, to give it more time to consider the case. During this time, William attempted to seek out the true murderer of his nephews. He found the accused in New Jersey, but the man simply denied all knowledge of Elizabeth Wilson, her twins and the tavern. Wilson attempted to find witnesses who could identify the man and connect him to his sister. He was successful but became bedridden around Christmas.

William lost track of time during his illness and was not able to return to Elizabeth until the day before her scheduled execution. William's only choice was to request a second reprieve. He had to ride from Chester to Philadelphia and speak with a number of officials before eventually receiving a postponement. The officials were even leaning toward giving Elizabeth a full pardon. On the ride back, though, the Schuylkill River flooded and was running dangerously high. No bridges remained intact, and the ferry operators, despite William's pleas, were unwilling to risk crossing the river for any amount of money. The courageous William, knowing that his sister's life was in danger, plunged his horse into the river in a valiant attempt to swim across. The horse was killed in the crossing, but William managed to swim to the other side. Although he survived, the raging current had pushed him two miles downstream.

As the day of the execution arrived, the sheriff was forced to begin preparations for Elizabeth's execution. Thinking that a reprieve might

AMOS WILSON,
The Pennsylvania Hermit, who lived 19 years in a Cave.

A depiction of William Wilson in "Hummelstown Hermit" form from the pamphlet *The Pennsylvania Hermit. Courtesy of the University of Pittsburgh Library.*

THE

PENNSYLVANIA HERMIT.

A NARRATIVE

OF THE EXTRAORDINARY LIFE OF

A M O S   W I L S O N,

Who expired in a Cave in the neighborhood of Harrisburgh (Penn.),
after having therein lived in solitary retirement for the
space of nineteen years, in consequence of the
ignominious death of his sister.

ANNEXED,

Is the writings of Wilson while a recluse, and his reasons for
preferring a state of Solitude to that of the society
of his fellow-beings.

PHILADELPHIA.
SMITH AND CARPENTER, PUBLISHERS.
1839.

The cover of the pamphlet *The Pennsylvania Hermit* depicting William Wilson with the pardon too late to save his sister, Elizabeth. *Courtesy of the University of Pittsburgh Library.*

be on the way, he sent men along the road from Philadelphia who could signal if William was coming with a reprieve. Elizabeth was sentenced to die at midday, and when the appointed hour arrived with no sign of a reprieve, the executioner carried out the sentence. William arrived somewhere between several seconds and half an hour after Elizabeth died, depending on the version of the story being told. When he saw his sister, William ended his life as "William Wilson" and began his new life as the "Pennsylvania Hermit" or the "Hummelstown Hermit."

William receded from society and took to wandering South Central Pennsylvania. He preferred staying away from people when possible and took up residence in Hummelstown. His choice of residence turned him into a legendary character. William lived in a cave located in Indian Echo Caverns. The cave is a popular tourist destination today. In his spacious, reclusive cave, he slept and studied religion. Although he shunned human contact after the death of his sister, he would occasionally come out to trade for essential supplies. Today, his ghost haunts the cave.

The Legend of Joseph Crist

Nancy sat down with her grandfather after a simple meal of soup and sandwiches. He made himself comfortable in his favorite reclining chair, while she sat on the floor in front of the television. He asked her to turn off the television, and she knew by the tone of his voice that he was about to tell another one of his stories, probably one she had heard before. Her grandfather lit his pipe, leaned back, puffed a few times and began to speak:

Years ago, a stranger came to town. No one had ever seen him and no one would ever forget him. It was a beautiful Sunday morning in Wrightsville. Everyone was preparing for church services. I was only ten at the time and hated getting all dressed up in a suit and tie. Anyway, since it was so beautiful, my mother, little sister and I decided to walk to Sunday service. As we walked down the main street, we saw a man coming toward us, but the man wasn't dressed normal. In fact,

I remember thinking he was a criminal or a foreigner. My little sister, Betsy, was even more curious. She decided to let go of Mom's hand and question the stranger. Luckily, Mom was quicker than Betsy and yanked her away from the man. She scurried us off up the street, but I'll never forget the nervous look she had on her face.

The strangest thing about the man was his appearance. He had long, dark, unkempt hair, and he wore a tattered white robe. And he had no shoes on. He was walking down main street barefoot.

He kept walking and wouldn't you know old Mr. and Mrs. Clevanstine were coming from the other direction. Well, didn't the stranger just walk right up to them and ask them for a drink. Mrs. Clevanstine just shook her head and rolled her eyes. Mr. Clevanstine laughed and said, "Don't you think it's a bit early for a drink?" They both continued walking, while the confused stranger looked on.

As the stranger turned off Main Street and headed toward Locust Street, people were beginning to get curious. As he walked, heads poked out of windows and doors. Men and women stared, while the children laughed and pointed in mockery. No one knew who the stranger was, where he had come from, or why he decided to show up in Wrightsville, of all places.

Nancy's grandfather stopped his story for a moment, pausing to refill his pipe and think about what he was about to say.

Yep, this stranger sure did disturb the town that morning. People were talking all the way to church and didn't stop until the Reverend was walking down the aisle. It seemed as though everyone had made it to church that Sunday. There wasn't but two or three empty seats in the very back.

The Reverend began his sermon as usual, welcoming us and thanking us for coming. He began to speak about the time Jesus walked along the road with a crowd of Jews. He stopped at a well and asked a man for a drink from it. The man dipped a cup into the water, raised it to Jesus' lips, then threw the water in his face and laughed. Jesus stopped at two other wells along the way, where he was also refused a drink. As he walked, he passed the last well along the way. He decided to walk by the well, thinking he would be refused again. As he passed, the woman standing by the well came to Jesus and let him drink from the cup. She filled it again and again until his thirst was quenched. Jesus raised his head, looked into the woman's eyes and told her there would be a place waiting for her in heaven with Him. Then He turned and walked away.

As the Reverend was finishing the story, a voice spoke very softly from the back of the church. Heads turned, and I turned to see who was speaking. There standing in the very back of the church was the stranger. He was speaking about the story the Reverend had told. The stranger went into detail contradicting parts of the Reverend's story and emphasizing other parts.

Everyone stared in disbelief as the stranger walked slowly down the aisle. He stood in front of us and talked of peace and the grace of God. His words put the townspeople in a trance. They were so real, so true. He had a way of speaking that made you want to listen. Even the children went silent. He spoke for a long time, reciting the scriptures as if he had lived them.

Suddenly my mother turned to me and said, "It's Him, Jesus has come again." It was like a chain reaction as the rest of the congregation began to realize who this stranger really was.

As he walked up the aisle to leave, members of the congregation began to stand and follow. He walked out the doors of the church, turned and stared up at the tall building. Then he said, "We are inseparable." Then he looked at us, smiled and said, "And so shall it be with you. The church is a part of me and so should it be with you. Remember that."

He continued walking toward the river and the crowd that followed grew and grew. Suddenly, as we sat and listened to Him speak, sirens filled the air. They got louder and louder as they came closer to us.

Everyone turned to see why the car had stopped so close to us. Two men got out dressed in white suits and white shoes. They walked through the crowd toward the stranger, and my mother recognized them as hospital attendants.

The men stopped in front of the stranger said loudly, "Joseph Crist, we've come to take you back to the asylum. You know you've done a bad thing running away like that. Now we'll have to take extra precautions to keep you in line."

The attendants each took an arm of the man they called Joseph Crist and led him back to the car. Before he bent to get inside, I saw him smile and he turned to us and said, "Remember what I've told you, my people." Then he was gone.

The people began shouting in anger and shaking their fists after the car. I remember looking up at my mother and asking, "Mom, who was that man, and why did they take him away?"

Mother stood and stared after the car. She thought for a long time and finally said, "I know only one thing. His name is not Joseph Crist. I don't know why they took him away. That man does not belong in an institution. Many people fear things that interrupt their normal way of life. I think whoever locked that man up was frightened of him, maybe because they were confused, maybe because they couldn't understand or refused to try."

Nancy's grandfather leaned forward and looked at her. His look was intense, but his eyes were soft. Then he said to her, "Never be afraid of things you don't understand. Keep an open mind, ask questions, but don't judge others only by your standards."

Nancy thought about that for a long time. Her grandfather's story had really touched something in her. She sat back and wondered who the stranger really had been. Then she realized it didn't matter who he was—only that he had a message and he told it. And to those he told, they told others. That's what's really important.

LEWIS THE ROBBER

Throughout his life, David Lewis was a consistent scoundrel and thief, but in the one hundred years after his death, he became the Robin Hood of Pennsylvania. He stole from the rich to give to the poor, defended the needy and murdered no one. In only a matter of decades, David Lewis the criminal was transformed into Lewis the Robber, the folk hero. The name "Lewis the Robber" lives today in South Central Pennsylvania, even if the details of his deeds are vague. He's sometimes conflated with the "buried treasure" stories of the region, and newspapers often reference him just before tax day. (He supposedly gave impoverished widows the money to pay their taxes and then stole it back from the tax collectors.)

All in all, David Lewis was indeed a criminal, but not a very good one. He was caught more often than not, and his hauls were petty compared to the Wild Bunch Gang or the James-Younger Gang that operated later that century. The story of David Lewis breaks into three parts. First, there's the life of David Lewis, a small-time criminal and escape artist who spent most of his life on the wrong side of the law. Second, there's the David Lewis known through the *Confession or Narrative of David Lewis*, ironically much better known than David Lewis's real life. And third, there's the persistent folklore that has surrounded David Lewis since his death, turning him into a folk hero.

The bogus confession published following Lewis's death contended that he was born in Carlisle on March 4, 1790, but he was more likely born in Centre County in 1788, the youngest child of a family of twelve. The factual David Lewis may not have been a good man, and he was certainly not a good bank robber, but he was an excellent escape artist. Caught after deserting the United States Army during the War of 1812 and possibly waiting to hang, Lewis escaped Fort Niagara during artillery shelling that set the jail on fire. Imprisoned a second time for passing counterfeit bills and sentenced to six years of hard labor, he escaped once again. He was caught and returned to jail, but rather than having his prison sentence increased, the governor granted him a pardon, releasing Lewis three years early.

The editor of the *Carlisle Republican*, whose readership formed the community of Lewis's scams, was outraged: "Lewis is the same old offender, who was formerly convicted of counterfeiting Bank Notes and sentenced to the Penitentiary for a number of years, but who shortly after his confinement received the pardon of Governor Findlay in 1818, and was let loose upon society, to plunder and rob…Alas! We have fallen indeed on evil times when the pardoning power of the Executive is thus ignorantly and improperly prostituted to the dangerous purpose of liberating infamous cut-throats, robbers, and counterfeiters."

Unknown to the editor, Lewis had informed on fellow inmates looking to make their own escape and received an early release as a reward. Lewis's time in the good graces of the law was short-lived. By October 1819, he had returned to his nefarious deeds. Lewis and his gang robbed a man named McClelland as he road on horseback on the turnpike in Bedford County. Mr. McClelland alerted a nearby tavern, which formed a posse and caught Lewis. Imprisoned at the Bedford jail, Lewis escaped once again. Lewis and two co-conspirators burned a hole in the floor of the prison, dug a tunnel into the yard and then broke through the wall.

Unfortunately for Lewis, his escape just happened to coincide with one of South Central Pennsylvania's occasional October snowstorms, which aided his pursuers in tracking him down six to eight miles west of Bedford. Citizen volunteers put Lewis under a nightly guard. This noble but amateur guard was successful for almost two months. On December 16, John Connelly, who would be Lewis's partner in crime for the rest of his life, noticed a flaw in the bolt that held his irons to the floor. He managed to break off the bolt and then used the hefty bolt to break the irons of all of the prisoners. A newspaper account in the *Pittsburgh Gazette* at the time either began or captured a rising sentiment of the heroic Lewis:

> Lewis, the robber.—*Many little traits in the character of Lewis… are spoken of, and prove him to be a man of no common order. With all his villainy, there is something magnanimous in his conduct; there is every reason to suppose, that after Mr. M'Clelland was seized on the winding ridge, he owed his life to Lewis, as the others evinced an evident disposition to murder him. Whilst in jail in Bedford, a man of the name of M'Curdy was imprisoned for robbing a poor widow. Lewis made use of this fellow in extricating himself from his irons, but refused to let him escape with his company, swearing that any man who could rob a woman, was not fit to associate with gentlemen! M'Curdy was obliged to remain.*

We next find Lewis and Connelly attempting a home invasion at Mr. Beshore's house in eastern Cumberland County near Harrisburg. As unsuccessful as ever, Lewis was back in the Carlisle jail by the following morning. There had been a rash of Lewis the Robber sightings, and neighbors told strange tales of men asking about Mr. Beshore's finances. Mr. Beshore, certain that he was about to be robbed, set up a system to alert his neighbors if a robbery was in progress. When Lewis and Connelly attempted to force entry into his house, Mr. Beshore sounded a horn, and his neighbors rode to his assistance, saving Mr. Beshore and capturing Lewis. Connelly, however, escaped.

Although Cumberland County had a sound stone jail, Lewis's reputation as an escape artist was known by this time. Local authorities decided to transfer Lewis to the stronger Franklin County jail in Chambersburg. The Chambersburg jail held David Lewis securely for almost an entire month. Lewis and other prisoners concocted a plan to hide a string in the wall, drop it through the window and unbolt the door. The search for the convicts commenced in the middle of the night, but the posse found only Lewis's irons next to a chisel and an axe. The gang hid out for a month in the now famous cave at Doubling Gap, in what is now the Colonel Denning State Park. Caves purported to have hosted Lewis the Robber have become legendary throughout South Central Pennsylvania, but Doubling Gap is the only cave with documented evidence of Lewis's stay.

The gang, in cahoots with an innkeeper whose tavern was visible from the cave, communicated in code. If the innkeeper hung a white flag, all was clear and the gang was free to come out. If a red flag was out, danger was in the area. During this month, Lewis and his gang of escapees lived a life of pleasure, dancing with local girls and living off of local donations. When the gang split up on June 15, authorities captured Caesor, who gave up the location of his fellow escapees. Although all his information was accurate, by the time authorities made it to the cave, Lewis and the others had left. Lewis and Connelly attempted, and mostly failed at, a string of robberies between Cumberland and Dauphin Counties. Lewis and Connelly's fatal last stand took place in the borough of Driftwood in Cameron County at Samuel Smith's house.

As the sun was sinking in the evening sky, the posse came upon Lewis and Connelly at target practice. The posse told the convicts to surrender peacefully, but Connelly promised that he'd sooner "blow them all to hell." A fierce gunfight ensued. Lewis fell from wounds taken during the exchange. Connelly gave up, ran and hid in a tree. Later, the posse found that Connelly was also wounded. Brought to Mr. Carskadden's tavern in Lycoming County, Connelly succumbed to his wounds. Lewis made it all the way to the Bellefonte jail, but when he refused to have his arm amputated, he contracted gangrene and died on July 12, 1830. His *York Recorder* eulogy read:

> *David Lewis,* for the last time. *The notorious offender, the Robin Hood of Pennsylvania, died in the jail of Centre county, of his wounds, on the evening of the twelfth inst. in the 30th year of his age…Here we see, that the vengeance of offended justice, must sooner or later fall upon the head of the guilty. He was the terror of the mountainous parts of Pennsylvania, and even when apprehended always contrived some means of escape. But in his "present prison house, the grave," where neither bolts nor bars, but the strong hand of death holds him in detention, he is secure.*

In Pennsylvania during the years of David Lewis's life, pamphlets customarily accompanied executions chronicling the condemned's life, misdeeds and confession. The confession was often spurious, based on newspaper stories, court records and hearsay. Soon after his death, the *Confession or Narrative of David Lewis* appeared in the *Carlisle Republican*. The *Republican* knew that it needed to explain its uncanny, exclusive access:

> *Our readers will no doubt be interested with the following story of the unfortunate David Lewis, an account of whose capture and subsequent death, we have already published. It appears that time exhibited the most hardened indifference, and appeared confident of recovering from his wounds, but on being told by his physicians that a mortification was about taking place and in that case little hope could be entertained of his recovery, he began to manifest sincere marks of contrition and repentance. From this time till his death, he became very communicative, and at certain periods related to a gentleman who visited him in his*

prison, the annexed sketch of his life, and which we were told by the same gentleman, who handed it to us, is a true and correct statement of Lewis's own words. From its great length we find ourselves unable to crowd it in our columns this week, but shall endeavor to give the whole as soon as possible.

The *Republican* published the *Confession* in weekly installments but never made it to the end. The entirety of the text was published in a sixty-one-page pamphlet, of which only one original copy exists today, safely tucked away in the Library of Congress. The pamphlet was reprinted many times since then, each edition adding to, subtracting from or reworking the previous edition. Despite the interest in David Lewis's life, the *Confession* is largely a work of political satire, focusing its ire on Governor William Findlay.

The *Confession* puts David Lewis's birth in Carlisle in 1790 to a large family, poor but respectable. Lewis's father moved his family to Northumberland County when Lewis was three to take a job as a surveyor, but he died soon thereafter, leaving the family destitute. Lewis enlisted in the army but soon after deserted. He was caught, court-martialed and convicted. Sentenced to hang, his mother rode to the camp to plead for his life. The commanding officer took pity and commuted the penalty from death to imprisonment. Incarcerated in the Hessian Guard House at the Carlisle Barracks, Lewis used a knife to saw away at his hobbles, removed a wood plank from the cell floor and dug a tunnel to bypass the prison walls. He headed to a cave on the outskirts of Carlisle, known then as the Devil's Dining Room and often referred to today as the Lewis Cave. He then made his way toward his family in Centre County.

Hearing of the rash in upstart banks in South Central Pennsylvania, Lewis decided to try his luck at a related upstart venture: counterfeiting. Lewis was caught and jailed once again. But while the turnkey was at church, Lewis convinced a young lady named Melinda to free him. After his escape, Lewis married Melinda and settled with her for a brief time in New York. We see some of the chivalrous and noble outlaw traits that will later make Lewis the Robber legendary. He was considered a man "who robs a woman of her virtue, as a greater villain, and more of a robber, than he who follows the high-ways, and robs the rich man of his money." After swindling a few wealthy Princeton boys of their parents' money, Lewis returned to Pennsylvania, where the marks were more "credulous, ignorant, unsuspicious and easy to be imposed upon."

He considered kidnapping the banker Stephen Girard, thought better of it and returned to Bedford County and his counterfeiting schemes, but he was once again caught and imprisoned, this time at the Bedford jail. This is the same incident covered in the factual account of Lewis's life, but the *Confession* makes for interesting reading, due not to the similarities but the differences. Lewis had been sentenced to six years but only served three. During his three-year stay, he escaped once. The author of the *Confession* changed the sentence to ten years, of which Lewis served one, and the escape is not mentioned. The author used the *Confession* to indict Governor Findlay as a weak individual who granted pardons to criminals, not for providing the state with information but rather because he lacked a better constitution (the *Confession* debuted in an election year).

After Lewis's release, he headed to Bedford, where he robbed the aforementioned Mr. McClelland. He was no longer the leader and instead was merely "persuaded to join" in the robbery. Armed and drunk, the highwaymen waylaid Mr. McClelland. Deeming that it would be best to get rid of the witness, the gang prepared to kill Mr. McClelland, but Lewis defended him with his own life, promising that they would have to kill him too if they wanted to kill McClelland. Lewis explained that he had sworn to never take a man's life but in self-defense. Back in jail after the botched robbery, Lewis escaped, freeing all of the prisoners except for a man who had robbed a "poor widow" and was not permitted to accompany them. Lewis and company fled to the cave in Doubling Gap and then continued on to rob Mr. Beshore.

In the *Confession*, Mrs. Beshore, rather than Mr. Beshore, blows the horn to alert the neighbors. Escaping that time from the Carlisle jail, Lewis returned to the Doubling Gap cave and then went on to Carlisle, a homecoming of sorts. He slept the night in the courthouse, although unhappily, since he did not like being associated with any of Governor Findlay's institutions. Leaving Carlisle for their fateful journey north,

Lewis lamented losing a bundle of money in an alligator purse on the Juniata River, breeding a new Pennsylvania treasure legend. Before the shootout in Driftwood, Lewis had a fantastical run-in with a huge, two-headed snake. In the end, he asked for forgiveness, expressed concern for his family and thanked those who took care of him in his final days.

Although this document has lent much to the (mis)understanding of David Lewis, readers proclaimed it a fraud even at the time of publication. The *Bellefont Patriot* assured its readers that the *Confession* was pure fabrication and that David Lewis gave no final confession. So who wrote the confession? *Carlisle Republican* editor John McFarland and lawyer James Duncan, Cumberland County men who disliked Governor Findlay, are two good guesses. Either way, David Lewis did not write the *Confession*—that much is known. But since its publication in 1820, the *Confession*, partly based on Lewis's life and partly fabricated, became intertwined with oral tradition to create the legend of Lewis the Robber.

Now that we have finished with the historical David Lewis and the literary David Lewis, we can focus on by far the most interesting David Lewis: the folkoric David Lewis (or Lewis the Robber or, to the truly generous, the Robin Hood of Pennsylvania), collected from various sources. The following was first found in the preface to the 1853 edition of the *Confession or Narrative of David Lewis*:

> *The following incident is said to have happened in Mifflin county: Having failed of carrying into execution some of his deeply laid schemes for robbing several wealthy famers, during one of his marauding expeditions, and his finances getting uncomfortably low, he determined on making an effort to replenish at the first opportunity. Coming across a house that promised security from molestation, no other being near, he called at the door, and was admitted by an elderly female, of respectable appearance. Lewis, to ascertain where her money was kept, asked her to change a five dollar note. "That unfortunately I am unable to do," replied the woman, "for I have not a dollar in the house; and, what is worse," she added despondingly, as she caught a glimpse of a man coming through the woods some distance from the house, "there comes the constable to take my cow for the last half-year's rent.*

I don't know what to do without her." "How much is due?" inquired Lewis, hurriedly. "Twenty dollars, sir." "Have you no one to help you?" "No one," she replied. "Then I will," replied the robber as he drew from his pocket the exact sum, and threw it upon the table. "Pay that fellow his demand, and take his receipt, *but don't say anything about me." Lewis had just time to make good his escape unobserved, when the worthy official arrived. He was proceeding without more ado to drive away the cow, when the woman came forward, paid him the money and took his receipt. He immediately set out on his return, but had not proceeded far, when Lewis bounded into the road and accosted him with, "How d'ye do, stranger? Got any spare change about you?" "No!" simpered the frightened constable. "Come, shell out old fellow or I'll save you the trouble," returned Lewis, as he presented a pistol at him. This argument convinced the constable that the fellow was up to his business, and he handed over his money as quickly as possible. Lewis got his own twenty back, and forty dollars in addition. He often boasted that the loan of the twenty dollars was one of the best investments he had ever made.*

The following is from Elenore Loring Kinietz's "The Robin Hood of Pennsylvania" in *Keystone Folklore Quarterly*:

Another fine day a group of horseman came galloping wildly along one of the roads of Adams County. Ahead was a gentleman cantering at an easy gait as he idly flicked his whip. Plainly he was of the gentry who had little of importance on his mind except the delightfulness of the weather and his pride in his thoroughbred mount. Wheeling around him, the excited cavalcade asked early if he had seen anything of a fugitive. He gently replied that the road had seemed to be deserted, but that he merely had been ambling on a morning trip. His offer to join the chase was accepted and off they raced, leaving dust in their wake. After several miles the leader drew rein and decided to call it a day, for their mounts were tiring. The stranger smiled, lifted his hat, and said, "I trust you did not find Robber Lewis to be such a bad companion after all?"

Left: A vintage newspaper article referring to David Lewis as a "Modern Robin Hood" and including a legend about buried treasure. *Courtesy of the Archives of Pennsylvania Folklife and Ethnography.*

Below: The Chambersburg jail, which held David Lewis for almost an entire month before he escaped again. *Courtesy of the Archives of Pennsylvania Folklife and Ethnography.*

The following was told by Robert H. Lewis and published by Paul A.W. Wallace in *Pennsylvania, Seed of a Nation*:

One evening in the Bald Eagle Valley a Pennsylvania Dutchman, traveling alone with a good deal of cash in his pocket, found the falling shadows brought uncomfortable thoughts of Robber Lewis and the unwisdom of being caught at night in this peculiar haunt. He was glad to see a light shining from the window of a cottage, and he stopped to ask if he might have shelter for the night. He was made welcome, and the host pulled up a chair for him at a table where the cards were in play. Whiskey passing, his tongue became loosened, and he was soon

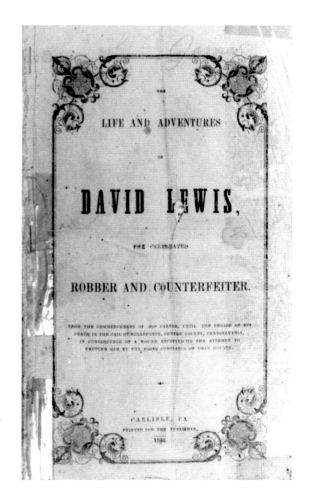

The oldest surviving copy of *The Life and Adventures of David Lewis, the Celebrated Robber and Counterfeiter* (1853). *Courtesy of the Archives of Pennsylvania Folklife and Ethnography.*

telling of his relief at finding shelter in the Lewis and Connelly country, especially considering what he carried in his pocket.

The evening passed pleasantly, he slept soundly, and he rose next morning refreshed and with pockets unlightened. As he said good-by to his handsome host, the latter wished him a safe journey. "You may tell your friends," said he, "that you passed a quiet night with Robber Lewis."

The following was collected by Nevin Moyer and first published by Mac Barrick in "Lewis the Robber: A Pennsylvania Folk Hero in Life and Legend" in *Midwestern Folklore*:

In Lewis' travels, one night he happened to stop with an old poor family. When supper time came, they had hardly anything to eat. The bed was alright but when breakfast was served it was about as scanty as the supper. Now Lewis saw they had a real good chicken house, a real good old log stable, but nothing in them. Finally Lewis bid the aged couple goodbye and thanked them for their amiable hospitality, but the aged couple were sorry that they could not entertain him any better but they said they did the best they could. Lewis left without letting the old couple know who he was, but he told them they will fare better in the very near future.

The day passed and so did part of the night, but by morning they thought they heard a great noise in their empty hen house. The venerable old man arose, went out to see what all the noise was, when to his great surprise, the hen house was filled with poultry. After that the aged couple did fare better and said their night lodger must have been Lewis the Robber, and he is the one that must have done this act of kindness.

Finally, the following was told by J. Raymond Bear and recorded by Eugene Utech in 1966:

An' another time, the Carlisle Fair was about due, an' Lewis the Robber was supposed to be walkin'. And there's a man come along, three or four race horses, ridin' one with a saddle. An' he was drivin' a flat wagon with sulkies on behind, goin' t' the Carlisle Fair. An' Lewis the Robber, he jist walked up, stopped the man, an' said, "Do ya mind if I ride along?" "No," he said, "I don't care." An' they jist got out in the country away from the mountain, he said to him, "Ain't you afraid to ride with me?" He said, "No, I know who I'm ridin' with." "Why," he said, "who?" He said, "Lewis the Robber." So they struck up a great conversation, an' he told 'im he was poor, and his horses wasn't good enough to win, and he jist thought aft'erds, "Well, there's no use 'n me to lie to 'im." An' he told Lewis the Robber, "I got good horses," 'n' he said, "I hit a lucky streak once 'n a while, but," he said, "I've got a wife 'n' family," he said, "I've gotta make a livin'." An' he said, "Okay," he said, "I'll keep ya in mind." So he never bothered 'im. He jist ignored him. If he did ever see 'im, he didn't hold 'im up.

THE WIZARD OF CUMBERLAND COUNTY

Mac Barrick was one of South Central Pennsylvania's most remarkable folklorists. His studies can be found in numerous folklore journals, including myriad entries in Pennsylvania Folklife. *But one essay that few people are aware of is his research into Daniel Drawbaugh, the "Wizard of Cumberland County." He wrote this remarkable essay as a senior in high school. The Hamilton Library and Historical Association of Cumberland County realized that it was a special essay and awarded it the Lamberton and Hamilton Library Association Prize in 1951. For the next half century, it sat tucked away in Mac Barrick's personal files. I reproduce here for the first time Mac Barrick's award-winning essay on the true inventor of the telephone, Eberly's Mills' Daniel Drawbaugh, as well as Barrick's never-before-seen hand-drawn sketches of Daniel Drawbaugh and his inventions.*

If we were to take a public opinion poll, asking the question, "Who invented the telephone?" to one hundred different people, perhaps eighty-nine would name Alexander Graham Bell, five wouldn't know, four would have no opinion, and at least two would answer Don Ameche [actor who played Alexander Graham Bell in *The Story of Alexander Graham Bell* (1939)].

Very few people know the actual inventor of the telephone, and for that reason, I'd like you to meet "The Wizard of Cumberland County."

One morning in the year 1876, there was unusual excitement in Eberly's Mills, a small hamlet about three miles southwest of Harrisburg in Cumberland County, Pennsylvania. Someone had broken into Daniel Drawbaugh's shop and stolen one of his inventions. "So what!" everyone thought. "He has so many foolish inventions. It probably wasn't worth anything."

Daniel Drawbaugh's entire life centered around Eberly's Mills where he was born July 14, 1827. Eberly's Mills was a town of many mills and shops. In addition to two mills and a machine shop, the town had a blacksmith shop and a gun shop, Daniel's father being a noted gunsmith of the town.

Most of Daniel's education was received in his father's blacksmith shop, since he was not particularly anxious to attend the Cedar Grove county district school, especially after he had been flogged for making a windmill that operated excellently but disrupted the class with its shrieking noise. Early in his life Daniel portrayed the inventive genius that had been handed down to him from his ancestors. His grandfather had been a blacksmith and now Daniel was fast becoming an expert machinist, in his spare time contriving things from the scrap iron that fell from the anvil.

Throughout his life, Daniel Drawbaugh received more than 125 patents from his some five hundred "scrap-iron" inventions. When he was only sixteen years old, he received his first patent, for an automatic sawing machine. Many wood-working devices and pneumatic tools poured from Drawbaugh's shop in rapid sequence. He invented a tack machine and improved the design of the tacks. Some people say he even built a sort of airplane in his shop, and not being able to remove it through the shop doors, he had to tear down the shop to get it out. In the field of photography, he constructed his own camera and fitted the lenses. He even improved the methods of enlarging pictures. Drawbaugh was a pioneer in placing insulation on electric wires.

As a boy he had studied electricity in night school under the tutorage of S.B. Heiges, who later became the superintendent of the public schools of York County and principal of the Cumberland Valley State Normal School. Fascinated by the wonders of electricity, Drawbaugh decided to devise ways to put it to work and so turned his attention to electrical machinery. He built an electric clock that stood six feet high and had a pendulum weighing forty pounds. Drawbaugh's clock was "the nearest thing yet to perpetual motion." Even in later years when Daniel was not able to work in his shop, his magnificent clock lost only two minutes in all the changing temperatures. Daniel Drawbaugh had a plan that would have furnished cheap electrical power for all of the Cumberland Valley. His plan to run transmission lines up through the valley and utilize the waterpower at every dam on the Conodoguinet and Yellow Breeches Creeks would have been very successful, but his "doubting-Thomas" neighbors, disapproving of the way he sometimes neglected his family, paid no attention to what they thought to be pure foolishness. "A man with a wife and children should be out working to support them instead of wasting his time in that old shop with these 'electrical experiments,'" they thought.

Mac Barrick's sketch of Daniel Drawbaugh, the "Wizard of Cumberland County." *Courtesy of the Archives of Pennsylvania Folklife and Ethnography.*

Some of Drawbaugh's Earlier Instruments

TEACUP TRANSMITTER
(1866)

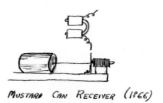

MUSTARD CAN RECEIVER (1866)

JELLY · GLASS TRANS-
MITTER
(1867-68)

AN EARLIER RECEIVER
(1869-70)

Above: Mac Barrick's sketches of four of Drawbaugh's earlier instruments, the "Teacup Transmitter," the "Mustard Can Receiver," the "Jelly Glass Transmitter" and "An Earlier Receiver." *Courtesy of the Archives of Pennsylvania Folklife and Ethnography.*

Opposite page: Mac Barrick's sketches of Daniel Drawbaugh's "Drawbaugh Phone," "Perfected Receiver" and "Perfected Transmitter." *Courtesy of the Archives of Pennsylvania Folklife and Ethnography.*

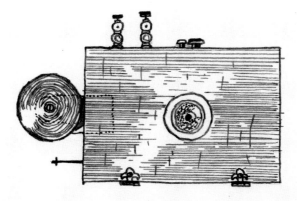

The Drawbaugh Phone (Aug. 1876)

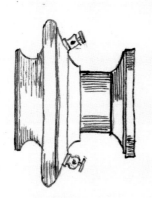

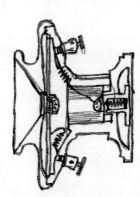

THE PERFECTED RECEIVER (1875-76)

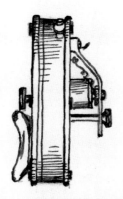
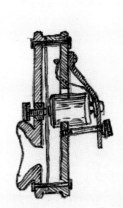

THE PERFECTED TRANSMITER (1874)

However, Daniel Drawbaugh's electrical experiments led him to develop one of the greatest single inventions the world has ever seen—the telephone. He was experimenting in this field as early as 1861. His first transmitter was made from a teacup and his earliest receiver was fashioned from an empty mustard can. He continued working on and improving his devices until in 1867, he succeeded in constructing an instrument that would convey the human voice. Because of a lack of money he was unable to obtain a patent for his invention at the time, but he did, nevertheless, demonstrate it to his friends and neighbors.

Several years later a certain Alexander Graham Bell, who had also been experimenting with the idea, heard of the invention and came to look at it. He studied Drawbaugh's models and discussed the construction of them with the inventor. About this time one of Daniel Drawbaugh's telephone models was stolen from his shop. On February 14, 1876, Alexander Graham Bell received a patent for a telephone that was actually the invention of Daniel Drawbaugh. Drawbaugh's later inventions and perfections on the telephone were protected by G. Milton Bair, Drawbaugh's representative in Washington, who had formed a rival company to that of Bell. Bell filed an injunction against the Drawbaugh Company. The case was taken to the United States Supreme Court, and eight years of litigation followed during which time more than 200 witnesses spoke in Drawbaugh's favor testifying that Drawbaugh had a speaking telephone long before Bell discovered the idea. Nevertheless, the Supreme Court voted four to three in favor of Bell. After the trial, one of the dissenting justices made the statement, "Bell never transmitted an intelligible word through an electrical instrument until after his patent." Alexander Graham Bell himself admitted that this was true. So ended the Bell-Drawbaugh case. Even though Daniel Drawbaugh lost his case, it was proved in the Supreme Court of the United States that he had a telephone in mind as early as 1861. Much time and money were lost in the trial including the $1,100,000 that had been offered to Drawbaugh to settle the case out of court.

The great inventions and marvelous discoveries of Daniel Drawbaugh placed him in a class with such great inventors as Michael Faraday,

Thomas Edison, and Benjamin Franklin, and yet he died November 9, 1911, after eighty-four years of hardship, disappointment, and poverty, in Camp Hill, Pennsylvania, "unwept, unhonored, and unsung."

THE PERFORMO TOY COMPANY

Middletown, Pennsylvania, is a small borough of nine thousand residents located nine miles southeast of Harrisburg, the state capital. Although it has a proud history of its own, marked by the occasional plaque, the town is more remarkable for how often it is overlooked. Middletown boasts features unheard of in most small towns. It's home to a Penn State campus, one of the largest in the state—Penn State Harrisburg. Middletown has its own international airport—Harrisburg International Airport. Even its name is quotidian. In 1929, when Robert and Helen Lynd needed a generic name for Muncie, Indiana, one that could be representative of any typical town, they chose Middletown. It was a good choice. If we combine the Middletowns and Middletons of the United States, the forty-seven of them come second only to the forty-nine Greenvilles of the United States. Not that Middletown's name is often used. In the Harrisburg region, there are signs for Lancaster, Hershey and York but rarely for Middletown. The way to Middletown usually just reads "Airport."

Middletowners are aware of the slights and will put up with the occasionally radioactive joke, but they have a communal source of pride as well: the Performo Toy Company, the original inventor of Mickey Mouse. In Middletown, a legend ostensibly about corporate treachery serves instead as a valuable reminder of the vital contributions of the oft-overlooked. Performo was the brainchild of two South Central Pennsylvanians, Torrence Dietz and Rene Grove. Dietz was a lumber salesman from Harrisburg who usually had extra wood, and in 1925, he also had extra cash. Grove was an artist from Middletown with a talent for toy making but who was short on cash. Grove was particularly fond of action-oriented toys—moveable, poseable and stackable. Before partnering with Dietz, Grove had already invented two toys, the popular

Aug. 17, 1926.   Des. 70,840
R. D. GROVE
ANIMAL TOY
Filed June 3, 1926

Inventor
Rene D. Grove

By *Watson E. Coleman*
Attorney

The drawing from Rene Grove's patent for Micky, filed on June 3, 1926, and patented on August 17, 1926. *Courtesy of the United States Patent and Trademark Office.*

Patented Aug. 17, 1926.   **Des. 70,840**

UNITED STATES PATENT OFFICE.

RENE D. GROVE, OF MIDDLETOWN, PENNSYLVANIA, ASSIGNOR TO PERFORMO TOY CO., INC., OF MIDDLETOWN, PENNSYLVANIA, A CORPORATION OF DELAWARE.

DESIGN FOR AN ANIMAL TOY.

Application filed June 3, 1926. Serial No. 17,928. Term of patent 7 years.

To all whom it may concern:
Be it known that I, RENE D. GROVE, a citizen of the United States, residing at Middletown, in the county of Dauphin and State of Pennsylvania, have invented a new, original, and ornamental Design for an Animal Toy, of which the following is a specification, reference being had to the accompanying drawings, forming part thereof.

The figure is a perspective view of my animal toy.
I claim:
The ornamental design for an animal toy, as shown.

RENE D. GROVE.

The text from Rene Grove's patent for Micky. *Courtesy of the United States Patent and Trademark Office.*

"Joy Boy" (a poseable boy) and "Wadee-Nodee" (a duck on three wheels that wobbles when it's pulled).

Grove had a talent for innovative toys. Dietz had a knack for taking a product from one place and selling it in another—a job he had been doing with lumber all of his life. While Performo did sell locally, its primary distributor was in New York. Dietz's business acumen soon landed them a contract to produce wooden toys of Felix the Cat—the most popular cartoon character at the time and a guaranteed moneymaker. Performo expanded rapidly, requiring additional space and staff, but it always remained rooted in Middletown.

After a year of Red Cross service in France during World War I, Walt Disney returned to Kansas City, ready to begin a career as an artist. At Pesmin-Rubin Art Studio, Disney found a temporary job and, more importantly, a permanent friend, Ub Iwerks. When their temporary jobs expired, Disney and Iwerks decided to start a company of their own, the short-lived Iwerks-Disney Commercial Artists. While working at the Kansas City Film Ad Company, Disney took an interest in animated cartoons. He began showing Laugh-O-Grams in a local theater and started a second company, Laugh-O-Grams Studio. He hired solid talent like Ub Iwerks and Hugh Harman, and their cartoons proved popular, but Disney was a horrible financial manager, and the company went bankrupt.

A lesser man might have given up at this point, but Disney decided to start a third animation studio, this time in Hollywood. Walt and Roy Disney began Disney Brother's Cartoon Studio, first located in an uncle's garage, then behind a real estate office and eventually in their own building. They found some success through Alice Comedies, shorts combining live action and animation. New York distributor Margaret Winkler liked the sample Walt sent her and agreed to a deal for a whole series. Winkler then married Charles Mintz, who took control of the company. Disney had his greatest success to date in 1927 and early 1928. Oswald the Lucky Rabbit, created by Disney and Iwerks, was a hit. Flushed with success, Disney headed to New York in February 1928, hoping to squeeze out a few more dollars per Oswald short. Mintz then hit Disney with three humdingers: first, Mintz reduced Disney's salary per short rather than raised it; second, Mintz's company owned the rights to Oswald the Lucky Rabbit, not Disney; and third, Mintz decided that Disney soon wouldn't be needed at all, as Mintz had hired away all of Disney's animators, save the loyal Iwerks, who had refused, as part of a plan to start his own animation studio. Walt Disney had to find a new way.

Rene Grove made improvements on his popular "Joy Boy" design to create an anthropomorphic, fully poseable mouse, which he patented on August 17, 1926. The mouse had black feet; bendable arms, legs and a tail; and was usually black-and-white but occasionally other colors. The Performo Toy Company had dozens of toys for sale by this time—poseable, wheelable and stackable. The incredible popularity of the posable mouse caused a halt in production of these other toys. All efforts were focused on meeting the demand for this hot-selling rodent.

In an interoffice contest, all staff members submitted a name for the mouse. Torrence Dietz's brother, Lawrence Grove, having recently discovered the concept of alliteration, submitted "Micky" to harmonize with "mouse." He won. The toy was named "Micky" (just "Micky"; no "Mouse"), and a name sticker was added to Micky's chest. Performo received a patent for the name on August 17, 1926. Working with distributor George Borgfeldt & Company, Micky was sold in New York's toy stores and department stores and was also displayed at the Toy Fair, a massive convention held every February in New York. Times were never better for the Performo Toy Company.

In March 1928, Disney took the long train ride home from New York to Los Angeles, unavoidably passing through Middletown along the way. He lacked the new contract he desired, most of his old staff and his most successful character, Oswald the Lucky Rabbit. Within a month of returning to Los Angles, Disney was working on "Plane Crazy," starring his new character, Mickey Mouse. "Plane Crazy" was the first Mickey Mouse cartoon completed, but not the first released to the general public. "Plane Crazy" was a silent cartoon, and test groups despised it. They also hated his second cartoon, "The Gallopin' Goucho." Although he never lacked for confidence, Disney knew that his cartoons were missing something. At a screening of *The Jazz Singer*, the first feature-length film to employ synchronized sound segments, Disney had his epiphany: Mickey needed synchronized sound—music, sound effects and voices. Playing

UNITED STATES PATENT OFFICE

WALTER E. DISNEY, OF LOS ANGELES, CALIFORNIA

DESIGN FOR A TOY OR SIMILAR ARTICLE

Application filed October 30, 1929. Serial No. 33,219. Term of patent 14 years.

The text from Walt Disney's patent for Mickey Mouse. *Courtesy of the United States Patent and Trademark Office.*

To all whom it may concern:

Be it known that I, WALTER E. DISNEY, a citizen of the United States, residing at Los Angeles, in the county of Los Angeles and State of California, have invented a new, original, and ornamental Design for a Toy or Similar Article, of which the following is a specification, reference being had to the accompanying drawing, forming part thereof.

Fig. 1 of the drawing is a front elevation of my new design, Fig. 2 is a back elevation showing my improved design, and Fig. 3 is a plan view of the toy design embodied in this invention.

I claim:

The ornamental design for a toy or similar article substantially as shown.

WALTER E. DISNEY.

before the feature-length and now-forgotten *Gang War*, "Steamboat Willie" was a huge hit, and Mickey Mouse was an overnight sensation. The rumbles were even felt 2,500 miles across the country in Middletown, Pennsylvania, at least according to legend.

So where did Mickey Mouse come from? Although defenders of Disney will often decry Performo Toy Company's legend as "folklore," Disney's accounts are no less folkloric. Let's first look at Walt Disney's creation narrative. The most well-known of Mickey's creation stories comes from Walt Disney himself. Disney, depressed and down on his luck after his doomed trip to New York, took the train back across the country, necessarily passing through Middletown on the way. Sketching on the train, a stroke of genius led to the creation of Mortimer Mouse. Sitting at his side, Mrs. Disney loved the mouse but hated the name. Heeding the warning that no child would take to a Mortimer, "Mickey" Mouse was born. This is the most romantic of the creation legends: a pioneering animator heading west across the continent, down on his luck, develops an enduring character out of a solo stroke of genius.

This version is seconded by Disney's 1930 Mickey Mouse patent, which lists him as the sole creator. This may not confirm the account, but it might hint at why Iwerks became dissatisfied and chose to leave Disney the same year. In the opinion of the Disney Archives, the creation of Mickey Mouse was a joint effort between Disney and Iwerks. One legend states that Iwerks reworked an old sketch of a pet mouse that Disney used to keep in the studio. Another notes that Iwerks got the idea from an old Hugh Hafner drawing: a sketch of Disney surrounded by mice. Of the possibilities, Walt Disney's version is most relevant to the Middletown legend.

The earliest documentation of the Middletown legend is found in 1931 in the *Old Home Week Souvenir*. It states simply and briefly:

> *In 1926 the Performo Toy Company created the original "Micky Mouse" which is known to many millions of people throughout the world. At one time, their factory of 7500 square feet of floor space was working to capacity almost day and night and still could not keep up to the demands for Micky. The toy Mouse is still being made along with 40 other toys including character toys seen in the comic strips of the Sunday and Daily Papers.*

It includes the essential motifs but leaves out many of the details that latter-day legend-tellers embellish, once Performo Toy Company is bankrupt while Disney remains a household name. There are two ways the Middletown legend is most often performed. In its briefest version, the legend is purely visual, juxtaposing a Performo Micky toy or patent with an early Disney Mickey drawing. Performo's Micky is dated 1926; Disney's is usually between 1928 and 1930. This version's power is based on the similarity of the images, the similarly of the names and the indisputability of the patent dates. It can be appreciated by anyone and is the version most often found on the Internet and discussed by non-Middletowners.

The second version is the full narrative. This is the version longtime Middletowners tell. Although full of variation, it includes the following three-part structure. First, Walt Disney crossed paths with Performo's Micky, sometimes while in New York meeting with Mintz and sometimes while passing through Middletown on the train ride home. Larry Grove's version claims that Disney saw Micky "on display in a store" while "on a business and pleasure trip to New York with his bride." Robert Watts places the meeting at a February 1928 Toy Fair, held for people in the toy industry. Elmer Overdeer claims that "Disney admitted his idea came from seeing Performo Toy Company's Micky at the Middletown train station." The second part of the legend is constant. Disney turns Micky into Mickey Mouse. The final part explains the litigation or threat of litigation, which also varies quite a bit. Take for example Larry Groves's rendition of the legend:

Folk Heroes and Legends

Walt Disney was reported to have made a business and pleasure trip to New York with his bride. While there, he took the idea back home. He placed an "e" in the name. A lawsuit was filed, but the little company was no match for the big corporation. Performo Toy folded. At least we can be thankful…to the Disney corporation for making animated movies of the mouse for entertainment for all nationalities around the world.

The motif of frequent litigation is central to the legend and easily misinterpreted. The regular occurrence of the theme is also notable considering that it's highly doubtful that there ever was any litigation. The History Channel claims that it did a nationwide search and was unable to find anything. The Disney Archives claims that it has no records of litigation for or against the Performo Toy Company, and Metzer Wickersham Kraus, Performo's legal counsel, destroyed all of its records in the 1950s. So why is this part always included in the legend? It seems to refer to the inevitable defeat of the little guy at the hands of the moneyed corporation, a worldview that fits well in little Middletown. While on the surface this part seems to be about corporate treachery, it is actually a persuasive device confirming the rest of the legend. Whether Performo sued Disney, Disney sued Performo or Performo merely drowned under mounting litigation costs, the real purpose is in confirming the value of Performo's Micky, and thus, the legend. If Performo's Micky was the real deal, it seems to say, a lawsuit would be required, even if defeat at the hands of a wealthy corporation was inevitable.

Rene Grove, Torrence Dietz and the other Performo Toy Company investors never seemed as interested in Disney as the latter-day legend-tellers are, and perhaps for good reason. Walt Disney today is an American icon, synonymous with both happy childhood memories and corporate America. Almost all of the legends about Performo Toy Company reflect that particular Walt Disney—a Disney who differs very much from the Walt Disney of 1928. The Disney whom Rene Grove and Torrence Dietz saw was a kid in his mid-twenties, only recently out of his uncle's garage, and always on the brink of bankruptcy. Performo Toy Company was a successful business as well, and no one could have predicted how long-lasting Mickey's popularity would be. Felix the Cat and Oswald the

Lucky Rabbit had faded quickly. Who would have thought that Mickey Mouse and that Walt Disney kid wouldn't do the same? The legend became more appealing later when the Walt Disney at the pinnacle of his career could be conflated with the 1928 caper, and Mickey Mouse could truly be seen as a great heist. It was in the 1930s, when Performo had folded and Walt Disney was winning Academy Awards every year, that the legend became worth telling in Middletown. The continued success of the Disney Company encourages the continued telling of the legend and the maintenance of its underlying message.

And what is that message? It's not a message of corporate treachery. In Middletown houses, Performo's Micky stands on the shelf next to Disney's Mickey, while Middletown children sit entranced by the *Little Mermaid* or the Wonderful World of Disney's Saturday morning cartoons. The message, rather, is a reminder of the valuable contributions of the oft-overlooked. No one claims that Rene Grove and Torrence Dietz, left to their own devices, could have made Mickey the star that Disney did. Rene Grove created Mickey. Disney made him a star. If there's any hint of continued condemnation, it's for the hypocrisy of Disney, so protective of his intellectual property rights while disregarding the rights of others.

But really, at its heart, it's a confirmation of value. Big ideas can come from little places. Middletown may not get its name on the road signs, the airports or the universities, just like Performo Toy Company won't get its name in the official annals of Disney history. Overlooked and unacknowledged every day, Middletown contributes to the Greater Harrisburg area. Middletown knows this, even if others don't. Overlooked and unacknowledged, this little town contributed to one of the greatest pieces of popular culture in the twentieth century. Middletown knows this, even if others don't.

Part III

MURDEROUS MEN

JOHN HARRIS AND THE MULBERRY TREE

The legend of John Harris and the Mulberry Tree is one of the oldest in Dauphin County. The attempted burning by drunken Indians followed by a heroic rescue, possibly led by his slave Hercules, makes for great drama. Myriad versions of the legend circulate, both in oral tradition and in print. My favorite version is found in the John Harris–Simon Cameron Mansion. Asked repeatedly about the legend, John Harris's great-great-grandson Philip Harris decided to record the legend for posterity. The original manuscript is framed and hangs on the second floor of the mansion.

My Great, Great Grandfather John Harris of Yorkshire, father of the founder of the City of Harrisburg, Penn., came to America with his personal friend William Penn in 1683 and brought this clock with him, and it has been in the Harris family ever since, except a few years when it was in the care of the Supreme Council 33° A. & A. Scottish Rite Masons at Washington, D.C.

It has come to me as his last living male representative. About the year 1720 a party of intoxicated Indians came to the house of John Harris on the bank of the Susquehanna River where the city of Harrisburg now stands and demanded Rum. Fearing mischief he refused to give it

Left: This woodcut by G. Gilbert from the cover of an 1840s almanac depicts the Indians as drunk and murderous. In the background, Hercules leads the friendly Indians to save his master. *Courtesy of the Historical Society of Dauphin County.*

Below: This watercolor exists in at least two versions. One depicts the attempted burning of John Harris from a distance. The second is the same painting, except without the Indians, making for a much more bucolic scene. *Courtesy of the Historical Society of Dauphin County.*

Opposite bottom: John Harris asked to be buried next to the legendary mulberry tree. The tree washed away years ago, but the grave still stands. *Courtesy of the Historical Society of Dauphin County.*

Sinclair's lithograph titled *The Rescue of Harris* actually shows little in the way of a rescue. The Indians look to be calmly and efficiently building his funeral pyre. The specks on the Susquehanna in the distance may be the rescue party. *Courtesy of the Historical Society of Dauphin County.*

to them. This enraged the Indians and they bound him to a Mulberry tree, with the avowed intention of torturing and burning him. Thro' the instrumentality of his Negro slave Hercules a party of friendly Indians were brought to his rescue. They came just in time to prevent the flames reaching his body.

John Harris immediately set Hercules free. In grateful remembrance of this interposition of Divine Providence, he requested to be buried at the foot of the Mulberry tree, and there he lies in "Harris Park" in the City of Harrisburg Penn., on the bank of the Susquehanna River, immediately in front of the Stone Mansion built in 1766 by his son John Harris Jr., with his wife, some of his children and the Negro Hercules. A portion of the trunk of the tree stood over his grave (say two feet high and eleven feet in circumference) until some years ago when it was overthrown by a flood.

John Harris died on December 1748, a faithful member of the Church of England.

BLACK JOAN

The Hart family, operators of Hart's Log Trading Post, lived near Tussey Mountain along the north side of Elk Gap, on the Martinsburg side. Their young daughter, Joan, loved to travel through the forests and mountains. Her father traded with the Indians, and his long business trips to distant Indian villages kept him away from home most of the time. Because he was away so much, he bought his family a rifle for protection and for hunting while he was away. Joan was beautiful, but beneath her beauty hid a vicious temper.

One day, while Joan was tramping through the mountains, she came across a saltlick placed by Indians to draw wild game. Since Joan always dressed in black, she easily concealed herself in the thick brush and pines. A large deer came to the saltlick. As it was enjoying the salt, Joan put the deer in her crosshairs, but before she could shoot, a hidden Indian took the deer for himself. Feeling that the Indian had taken what was rightfully hers, she turned her gun on him instead.

No one else was around, and Joan decided to keep the incident to herself. Later going back to the saltlick, Joan drove spikes into a pine tree so she could hide and watch the saltlick from an elevated vantage point. From May to November 1776, Joan traveled to her tree to hunt. Her black dress always kept her safe and invisible in the dark forest.

When her father returned, he told her to be careful roaming the forest and to stay away from the saltlick. A number of his Indian friends had been killed there over the past few months. The Indians were searching for the man who had killed their tribesmen but had found no one as of yet. When they did, though, they would hang the man by his arms and fill him with arrows, her father assured her.

The girl confessed to her father that it was she who had been killing the Indians. Even after he found the skeletons of fifteen Indians underneath her bed, her father kept Joan's murderous deeds a secret until sixteen years after Joan died—the unnatural death of a hateful heart.

THE BLUE-EYED SIX AND THE MOONSHINE CHURCH

In 1879, six men in Indiantown Gap conspired to murder indigent Joseph Raber, hoping to cash in on their insurance policy. A hired man murdered Raber. A witness saw the murder, and police (assisted by the insurance company) unraveled the conspiracy. The popular press noticed that all six conspirators had blue eyes, which caught the imagination of the general public. A jury convicted the men, who were hanged at a local prison and buried at their family cemeteries. Their victim, Joseph Raber, was buried at the Moonshine Church. Over the years, the various aspects of the legend have been conflated to the point where it is popularly believed that the six men were hanged at the Moonshine Church Cemetery and subsequently buried there. In many versions of the legend, their twelve blue eyes—the most memorable image from the legend—haunt the Moonshine Church Cemetery:

> *Well the way I remember it, these six guys all with blue eyes; that's how they got the name the Blue-Eyed Six. Well they all decided to kill*

this man, a guy named Drew. And the leader of the six, his name was Brandt. I remember his name, 'cause the guy next door had the same last name. Anyway these six guys decided to kill him for insurance money, so they drowned him at St. Joseph Springs, Indian Town Gap. I don't know what they meant by insurance money, but that's what everyone said. Anyway these six guys were caught, tried and sentenced to the gallows. After they were convicted, all of 'em were hung right down here on S. 8ᵗʰ Street. That's the way I remember the story…

Yeah I remember the story of the Blue-Eyed Six; they drowned a man up at Indian Town Gap. Don't know why it took six of 'em. Ya see, these six men all had blue eyes. That's how they got their name. And they killed this guy because of all the money he had. That's the way I understood it. Well it didn't matter anyway, because the police caught all of 'em. All six of 'em were hung here in town. Down on 8ᵗʰ Street I think. Served 'em right, they shouldn't have killed the poor man…

The Moonshine Church and the Moonshine Cemetery are the locations for much of the Blue-Eyed Six legendry. The murderers are said to have been hanged and buried here when, in reality, only the victim Joseph Raber is buried here. *Courtesy of the Archives of Pennsylvania Folklife and Ethnography.*

Yes, I remember the story the Blue-Eyed Six fairly well. First off the gang got their name because all the fellas in cahoots had blue eyes; which struck me as very odd, don't know why, I just always though it was kind of queer. Anyway these six guys killed a man named Drew or something like that. I heard they drowned him, but I'm not really sure about that. I think the reason they killed this man was because he had a whole lot of money. Anyway all six of them were caught and I think all of 'em or most of 'em were hung for it. I'm pretty sure they were all tried right here in town for the murder…

This church, called Moonshine Church, was out near the race track I used to work at as a teenager. The church was off in the woods on the mountain and everyone said that it was haunted. Supposedly six Indians were hung out at the church back during early America. The settlers hung the Indians because they all had blue eyes. Supposedly in the woods around that area, late at night, you can see the blue eyes of the Indians haunting the woods…

THE BROAD MOUNTAIN TORCH MURDER

On Palm Sunday in April 1925, Mr. and Mrs. Claude Duncan took a walk over Broad Mountain near their hometown of Gordon, Pennsylvania. Just off the road, they stumbled upon the burned body of a young woman. Police never solved the crime, which became the basis for the Broad Mountain Torch Murder legend. An autopsy showed that the young woman was semiconscious when she was doused in gasoline and burned alive. Her clothing, hair and the surrounding grass were all burned, suggesting that she died at the location. The Pennsylvania State Police investigated the case but had few substantial leads. They found the gas station that sold the five-gallon can of gasoline but little else. Police preserved the woman's head in alcohol and made a plaster cast of her face for identification.

When word of the crime spread, parents and relatives of missing young women visited the small village to view the plaster cast, hoping to find their own missing loved one. No one ever identified the victim, but the speculation was intense. Because of the proximity to several bawdy houses, some thought that the young woman was a prostitute. Others speculated that she was a runaway or an escapee from a mental institution. Still others thought that she was a city girl caught outside of her element. In small-town Gordon, everyone had a favorite theory, and everyone talked.

Shortly after the gruesome discovery, nighttime motorists along the lonely mountain road reported that their headlights would go out and their car engine would stall near the site of the murder. They blamed the ghost of the young woman as the cause of their car trouble, although most did not claim to see an apparition. The number of sightings and reports of incidents grew until hundreds of cars gathered each night hoping to see something. Some nights, a mist formed over rain puddles, and the crowd would experience a "ghost" rising in front of them, leaving the crowd convinced that they had indeed seen a spirit.

During the summer of 1925, three boys—J.A. Seitzinger, Claude Duncan and Steve Secunda—decided to add to the excitement. They attached a white dress and a mannequin's head to a rope, which they threw over a tree limb. One boy hid and waited, while the other two guided a group near the spot. The hidden boy pulled the rope, making the "ghost" appear. The boys had a great summer pulling the prank, and the belief of a "spirit" on Broad Mountain spread further than ever.

Virginia Yarnell presented a paper to the Schuylkill County Historical Society in the mid-1970s on the events that took place on Broad Mountain in 1925. In her essay, she laid out the facts that were available and spoke on the early formation of the legend. Yarnell told Steven Boyer in an interview, "When this thing happened, no one had TV and more families spent time together walking. I was only one-year-old, and my parents almost went with the Duncans that morning. The story was always exaggerated, and the ghost was nothing but a fake. Many people still swear that their cars still stall at the spot and that sometimes 'something' is seen there."

When the "visits" to the murder site truly became "legend trips" is open to speculation. In the beginning, curious visitors wanted only to view the scene of a grisly murder. Later, as more and more adolescents began to explore the area nearby, the location became a traditional teenage legend trip. Because the whole of Broad Mountain is rich in anthracite coal and heavily mined, the area contains a vast system of dirt roads that run the length and breadth of the mountain. Teenagers traveled these roads to reach remote mountain locations, perfect for underage drinking and parking.

Teenagers still set out to find the ghost of Broad Mountain. Playing off the fact that the state police have the victim's preserved head in storage, one legend says that on nights when the moon is full the lady roams Broad Mountain searching for her lost head.

One legend tripper remembered her group planning the trip at the beginning of the month because they knew that the moon would be full. The whole group got extremely excited talking and telling stories, wondering if the car would stall when they got to the spot of the murder. The planning and storytelling turned out to be more exciting than the

John Joy of the Schuylkill County Historical Society holds the cast created after the Broad Mountain Torch Murder in hopes of future identification. *Courtesy of the Archives of Pennsylvania Folklife and Ethnography.*

actual trip. Regardless, she remembered that it was a big event in her life. One of the boys remembered how fun it was to take girls up to Broad Mountain. They would be so frightened they would fight to sit near him. What could be better?

CAMP SHIKELLAMY

Camp Shikellamy's name comes from an old Indian legend. A squaw and a brave lived in the mountains north of Harrisburg near Fishing Creek Valley. In winter, the harsh mountain climate made hunting difficult, and the tribe was no stranger to hunger. For over a week, the brave hunted for game to feed his family, but every day he returned home empty-handed. On the morning of the ninth day, wracked with hunger pains, the Indian squaw warned her husband not to return until he had found food for his family. The faithful brave set off once again, struggling through the frosty terrain. He scoured the mountains for hours upon hours, only to fail to find food once again. He trudged, freezing and hungry, back to his starving family. As cold as the brave was from the failed hunt, his homecoming was even colder. When the squaw saw her husband returning empty-handed once again, she picked up a nearby log and tore after him. The brave sprinted away as fast as his legs would carry him, but his wife followed, eventually trapping him at the edge of a cliff. Without a moment's hesitation, the brave threw himself from the cliff, his words echoing through the mountains, "She killin' me! She killin' me!" And that's how Camp Shikellamy got its name.

THE OLD GIRLS' SCHOOL MURDERS

In 1890, an elderly groundskeeper took care of the Old Girls' School in Academia, performing odd jobs like painting and doing minor repairs. Most of the school's students came from distant towns and boarded on campus during the school year. No one ever paid much attention to the old man, and he began to feel neglected. One fall night, the old man snapped. He went to the school's toolshed and picked out the largest, sharpest knife he could find. He headed to the living quarters, where he chained all of the doors, and then made his way upstairs to the large room where the girls slept. Quietly, he snuck from bed to bed, slitting the girl's throats. Only one schoolgirl was alive when he reached the last bed. Instead of slitting her throat, he laid down his knife and just stared at her. The girl woke, and when she saw the deranged groundskeeper hovering over her, she let out a bloodcurdling scream.

The man snatched the girl up and took her into the attic. The next morning, the schoolmaster found the man and the girl hanging from the attic rafters. Part of the Old Girls' School still stands in Academia. Enter the building at night, journey to the scene of the crime and then stand silently and listen. On fall nights, visitors can hear the footstep of the old man padding from bed to bed and then hear his climb up the attic stairs, dragging the little girl behind him. Some say that on certain nights, you can even hear the last girl's scream.

John Wert

In 1920, Amish John Wert was plowing his field. The ground was hard, and he was having great difficulty controlling his team of horses. This was partly because some of the boys of his "English" (non-Amish) neighbors stood alongside the field, heaving rocks at him. These teenagers loved harassing John. One of the boy's stones found its mark, hitting a horse in the eye. The horse jerked and threw John Wert under the plow. The spooked horses pulled the plow over John, severing his leg. The boys ran off, leaving John Wert to bleed to death. The thick forestation on the road that runs through Wert Hollow, past John Wert's field, is dark even in the daytime.

One night a few years ago, several teenage couples had found the hollow an ideal location for fooling around away from prying adult eyes. The moon was full, the evening was warm and their car windows were down. Suddenly they heard a buggy winding down the road. Peering out their car windows, they saw nothing. The sound continued to approach, getting closer and closer, but still they could see nothing. It got to the point where it sounded like the buggy was headed straight for them. The noise grew so loud that the teenagers were sure they were about to be struck by a buggy. They heard the buggy slam into their car with a sickening crash. When they were able to rouse their courage and step out of the car to check the damage, they found their vehicle untouched. Plenty of people still travel to Wert Hollow, but only teenagers can hear John Wert's buggy. John Wert knows who needs to be repaid and who doesn't.

REDMAN

Redman lurks in the woods of Mount Gretna, where everyone knows his name yet nobody has ever seen him. Nonetheless, there is consensus on his physical description. He's a huge man, reddish from his Indian heritage. He carries an axe and is generally very frightening to witness.

While camping in the open in Soldiers Field in Mount Gretna, Greg heard Redman. It was a faint noise in the woods, followed by a flash of Redman's axe.

Albert, who lives in the camp meeting ground of Gretna, has seen Redman run by his house late at night. Although Albert knew Redman was there, he did not get a clear view of him.

Rick saw Redman while camping at the bottom of the Governor Dick fire tower. While vandalizing the tower, Rick and his friends heard Redman in the woods and halted their crime early. Because of his Indian heritage, Redman is known to intervene on behalf of nature in the Mount Gretna area.

Tap, Becky and Rachel recalled a story about Redman from their childhood. Their father owns the Gretna Timbers Restaurant and Dinner Theatre in Mount Gretna and would put the girls in the back of the station wagon while driving around doing his errands. One summer night, the girls were waiting for their father in the car. It was raining and they were frightened. Rachel heard scratching on the top of the car, and she knew that Redman was outside. Rachel and Becky froze, and Tap hid under an old dirty blanket in the back of the wagon until Redman had enough and decided to leave.

The staff members at the Gretna Timbers Restaurant and Dinner Theatre often enjoy a rousing game of basketball after a hard day's work. If the basketball rolls into the woods, the person who cast the errant shot must retrieve it, which means he will be entering known Redman territory. As he sets out to reclaim his ball, the rest of the crew sends up the chant, "Redman, Redman, Redman."

Redman can also be found at midnight at Dinosaur Rock in the small town of Colebrook, where residents hear Redman rustling through the woods.

SUSSMUMMI

In Ringtown, there was a place where people would cart their ashes and trash and dump them over a cliff. Down in the valley beneath the cliff lived a lady named Sussmummi. Everyone in Ringtown believed that Sussmummi practiced powwow and hexed people. A young man lived with his father on a nearby hill overlooking the same valley. One day, the young man picked up a rifle and shot through Sussmummi's window, killing her on the spot. When the police arrested him, he explained that the reason he shot Sussmummi was that every month, when the moon was full, she turned him into a black cat. The only way he thought he could stop Sussmummi from hexing him was to kill her. The young man was tried and sentenced to prison. The legend of Sussmummi and her black cat is still told in Ringtown today.

SAGA OF THE WHITE LILY

Joseph Walton and Martin Brumbaugh published Stories of Pennsylvania *in 1897. The book attempted to use the legends of Pennsylvania to educate schoolchildren on the subject of Pennsylvania history. This legend, like a number of tales in this book, focuses on violent Indians and Indian captivity. South Central Pennsylvania was a frontier for much of its history, and although relations varied from tribe to tribe, the threat of Indian attack was real. We see that anxiety clearly here. One of the authors, Martin Brumbaugh, later became the twenty-sixth governor of Pennsylvania.*

Part I: Regina

On a sunny morning in the autumn of 1754, John Hartman rose early and gathered his wife and four children around him in his cabin home. He had come from Germany to the peaceful province of Pennsylvania, that he might earn enough to feed and clothe and shelter his loved ones. The cabin door was ajar, the sun lay like a level rule of light upon the rough but clean cabin floor. The faithful dog, Wasser, was asleep in the yard. The harnessed horses were eating their morning meal. A flood of song poured from a hundred birds astir in the overarching trees. The blue smoke curled lazily upward from the rude chimney, and was lost in the melting mists of the valley near where Orwigsburg now stands.

The pious Lutheran father took his great German bible, which he had carefully brought from the Fatherland, and read the morning lesson. Then they all knelt, and the good man prayed, "We thank thee, O Lord, for thy great care and love to us. We are glad for the light of a new day. Help us to live it right. We love thy book; we worship thy son, our Savior, and we pray thee to keep us this day from harm and danger. But not our will, but thine be done."

Then the breakfast was eaten thankfully and the plans for the day made. Mrs. Hartman and the youngest child, fat, chubby Christian, were to go to the mill, miles away, to get flour and to visit sick Mrs. Swartz. Mr. Hartman and George were to finish seeding the last field before the rains of autumn began to fall. Barbara and Regina were to stay alone in the cabin and "keep house." As Mrs. Hartman and her baby boy passed by the clearing, they called a cheery "good-by" to papa and George. Little Christian, sitting astride the old horse and held by his mother, waved a fond farewell as they passed into the forest.

At noon Barbara took the great tinhorn and gave a mighty blast to call the workers to dinner. While the family was eating, old Wasser came rushing into the house. Mr. Hartman knew his brave dog would not run from a common foe. He spoke to the dog; but Wasser stood in the door, his bristles up, growling fiercely. Then the dog made a fearful leap and landed upon a big Indian and brought him to the ground.

Mr. Hartman ran to the door. Two sharp rifle cracks rang upon the air. Two bullets from heartless foes struck the innocent man. He fell dead. George sprang to his father's side, and he too was struck dead. Then the Indians tomahawked faithful Wasser. Fifteen yelling, hideous demons rushed into the cabin. Barbara ran into the loft, but poor, sweet Regina threw up her hands to heaven, and cried, "Herr Jesus! Herr Jesus!" For a moment that name struck them dumb. Then they seized Regina, and drew a scalping knife over her lips to tell her to keep still. They dragged Barbara from her hiding place and made the poor girls serve to them the dinner they had so gladly and carefully set for Father and George.

As the girls gave food to the murderers of their loved ones, they could see their dead father and brother lying across the cabin floor.

As soon as the Indians had eaten everything to be had, they began to plunder the cabin. They tied in bundles everything they cared for, and taking Barbara and Regina by the hand, led them out into the field. Here the girls saw a dear, sweet little girl, only three years old, tied to the fence. When the little captive saw the Hartman girls, she began to cry bitterly, and say in German, "Oh, Mamma! Mamma! Where is my mother?"

While the children wept, the Indians set fire to the house, and as they led the sobbing children into the wilderness, the result of John Hartman's hard toil, together with his body and that of his son, disappeared in smoke.

Late that afternoon Mrs. Hartman returned, leading the horse. On its back was the grist from the mill and tired little Christian. When they came out of the forest Mrs. Hartman looked puzzled. No house was in sight. "Surely this is our place," she said to herself. Yes, there is the beautiful pine tree that stood close to our cabin. There are the fields, and there is the orchard, and there"—but her words were cut short by little Christian, who cried out, "Why, mother, where is our house?"

They hurried on. Then they saw the charred ruins of their happy home, and in the yard was blood. It was the blood of faithful Wasser. Then the awful truth—an Indian massacre—her loved ones dead or captives—came to her. She fell upon her knees and lifted her heavy heart to God in sobs and prayers. That night she went to a neighbor's house and told her story. News had also reached the place that a farmer named Smith had been murdered and his little child, Susan, carried off.

Poor Mrs. Hartman was almost wild with grief. In the ashes of her home the neighbors found the charred bones of Mr. Hartman and George, and a month later the body of Barbara was found by some hunters. Mrs. Hartman went to see the remains. It was only too true. The heavy tomahawk had done its work, and poor Barbara was dead. Under a large oak by a stream, with grief beyond control, the widowed and heart-broken woman laid Barbara to rest till the morning of the new day of God.

But what of Regina? "If I could only see Regina I would say, like good old Simeon, 'Now, Lord, let thy servant depart in peace.'" But no news came. Susan Smith and Regina Hartman were gone.

Years went by. Christian had become a strong lad of fourteen. He was his mother's only comfort, and did all that a noble boy could to make her days peaceful and happy. But how could she be contented while Regina's fate was unknown? When she read her Bible in the morning and knelt in prayer, she always asked God about Regina. In the evening hour, when the twilight settled about her lonely home and saddened her lonely heart, she would gaze far away into the fading western light and think of Regina:

> *Allein, und doch nicht ganz allein, bin ich*
> *In meiner Einsamkeit.*

> *Alone, and yet not all alone, am I*
> *In this lone wilderness.*

Would the black wilderness ever give her tidings of her dear child? We shall see.

Part II: Sawquehanna

In the dark woods of western New York, by the side of a mountain stream that leapt from the rocks and played with the sunbeams, stood an Indian wigwam. It was old and cheerless within, but grand and beautiful was the sylvan scene that faded into green and gloom around it.

Here dwelt an ugly old Indian woman, her son (a great warrior), and two girls who had been captives so long that they scarcely remembered their white parents. The older of these girls was Saw'-que-han'-na, "the White Lily"; the other was Kno-los'-ka, "the Short-legged Bear." The old squaw was called She-lack'-la, "the Dark and Rainy Cloud." And she was well named. The black forest, bending beneath the savage sweep of a mighty storm, was not so dreadful as Shelackla when she was crazed with rum. She beat these poor girls unmercifully, and they had lived for many years in great fear and greater suffering. They would often steal away into the forest depths, and, clasping each other around the neck, weep bitterly.

The great French and Indian War was fast drawing to a close, and the English were driving the French from America. Of all this Sawquehanna knew little and cared less. She had forgotten the language of her early home and had learned from the old squaw and her son to speak the Indian language. But when she sat alone for hours in tearful silence, her weary spirit longing for something, she knew not what, there would come to her dim memories of a happy home, a kind praying mother, the songs of the evening hour, and then the awful sense of fire, smoke, demons, death, and a long journey toward the setting sun. But of all this she could make nothing; and at last she would brush the tears from her eyes, dismiss the painful picture from her mind, begin again to grind the scanty store of corn, and patiently endure her hard and lonely lot. One day, in 1765, the soldiers of Colonel Boquet came to the wigwam of Shelackla and took the girls away. The war was over, and Colonel Boquet demanded "that all white children who had been taken captives by the Indians must be given up to the English government."

On September 13, all these children were gathered at Fort Duquesne, and anxious parents walked along the line, looked into each face, rushed forward with screams of delight, and clasped long-lost loved ones to their hearts. Old soldiers turned away and wiped the tears from their cheeks, and Colonel Boquet was so overcome that he wept like a child. But no one came for Sawquehanna. She and Knoloska and nearly fifty more were left weeping and wondering what all this meant.

Eight days later Colonel Boquet began a weary march with these children to Carlisle, hoping that there they might find father or mother and a home. For two weeks they toiled eastward, over the rugged mountains, through the fern-fringed valleys, by Fort Ligonier, Raystown, and Fort Louden to Carlisle. News of their coming had been sent ahead, and every family that had lost children hurried to Carlisle.

It was not long before people from the Blue Mountains picked out Knoloska as little Susan, the daughter of murdered Mr. Smith. It almost broke Sawquehanna's heart to give up her Indian sister. Susan clung to her and kissed her and wept. But they were no longer in the ugly old squaw's wigwam, and the officers promised Sawquehanna that she, too, might find friends, and perhaps they could again live together. But her heart was heavy. She made no answer, hung her head, and sobbed and moaned.

Poor old Mrs. Hartman, the mother of Regina, with little hope and increasing sorrow, left her mountain home, went by John Harris' Ferry, and came to Carlisle in time to see the tired children arrive. Mrs. Hartman looked into each face, hoping to find Regina; but no golden hair, no blue eyes, no ruddy cheeks like Regina's were there. As she turned to go away she saw Sawquehanna turn her bright blue eyes full upon her. But Mrs. Hartman walked on. Colonel Boquet came to the sad woman and said, "Can't you find your daughter?"

"No," was the answer given in sobs; "my daughter is not here."

"Are you sure? Are there no marks on your child by which you might know her?"

"None, Colonel; she was a perfect and spotless child."

"Did you never sing to your little girl? And is there no hymn that she was fond of?" "Oh yes!" was the answer; "I often sang her to sleep in my arms with an old German hymn we all loved so well."

"Well," said Colonel Boquet, "just sing that hymn as you and I walk along the line of girls. It may touch the right spot and give her to you again."

"It's no use, good man; she is not here, and besides, the soldiers will all laugh at an old German woman like me."

But the colonel pleaded on, and at last Mrs. Hartman began in a clear, loud, but tremulous voice to sing:

"Alone, and yet not all alone, am I
In this lone wilderness."

Everybody turned to look and listen. It was a touching scene. The pious old widow's hands were clasped in prayer. Her eyes were closed. Her snow-white hair made her upturned face fairly radiant, as the sun bathed her in light. When she sang the second line, a shrill, sharp cry was heard. It came from the heart of Sawquehanna.

In an instant she rushed to the singer's side, threw her bare arms around her neck, and sobbed "Mother"; and then Regina joined her mother in singing again the dear old song of their cabin home.

"Alone, and yet not all alone, am I
In this lone wilderness
I feel my Savior always nigh;
He comes the weary hours to bless.
I am with Him, and He with me,
E'en here alone I cannot be."

CHRISTMAS EVE MURDERS

On Christmas morning 2002, Jean Wholaver and her daughters, Victoria and Elizabeth, should have been opening presents beneath the Christmas tree. Instead, neighbors awoke to the twinkle of police lights and a house wrapped in yellow tape. Police found the three women dead, each murdered in a separate room of their house. Neighbors last saw the Wholaver family on December 23. The family had been expected in St. Benedict, Pennsylvania, on Christmas Eve. When they never arrived, their St. Benedict family called the police, who checked the house.

When no one answered, Sergeant Robert Givler of the Middletown Police Department entered the house on Christmas morning, finding the mother dead in the kitchen on the first floor as soon as he stepped into the house. An infant's wail brought him to the second floor, where he found Victoria, dead but cradling her nine-month-old daughter, Madison, who was alive and uninjured. Elizabeth lay in her bedroom, murdered in her own bed. Each had been shot a single time in the head with a .22-caliber weapon. The three had been killed the morning of Christmas Eve, with a light snow falling around the house. Although all three suffered gunshot wounds, neighbors heard no shots fired. Police immediately ruled out the possibility of random violence, citing the execution-style killings. Although denying he was a suspect at the time, police set out to question the girls' estranged father, Ernest Wholaver, who they were unable to immediately locate. Neighbors, on the other hand, were already certain of his guilt.

At the time, Ernest Wholaver was out on bail. The charge was years of sexual abuse against both daughters. In August of that year, fifteen-year-old Elizabeth had come forward, accusing her father of sexually abusing her since the fifth grade. Her case was strengthened by her older sister Victoria, an aspiring model who had kept quiet for years as her father molested her but came forward to support her sister, claiming that she had also been molested by her father. Victoria alleged that her father began molesting her when she was six years old and continued to do so for the next decade.

One of the conditions of Ernest Wholaver's $100,000 bail was prohibition from any contact with his wife or daughters and from possessing firearms. He could not return to the house and had been living in St. Benedict awaiting trial. Victoria Wholaver gave damning testimony at the August hearing: "One time my father took me upstairs and my mom had this set of lingerie or something. I don't really know what it was, and he like put it on me and put like lipstick on my cheeks and lips, and he made me look pretty and stuff. And then he, he made me have sex with him." Victoria said she never told anyone because she feared for her life. Her father was already cruel enough as it was, readily punishing his daughter for minor missteps. She testified, "I was scared to tell anybody about this because he told me that it would ruin his marriage and all that and then he said if I would ever tell anyone he would kill me." He had even put an unloaded gun to her head before.

Through threats and promised violence, Ernest Wholaver managed to keep his wife, Jean, unaware of the abuse going on under her own roof. The couple began divorce proceedings soon after. After the murders, other stories began to become public. Ernest Wholaver had put his young daughters to work, doing what neighbors referred to as "hard labor" while he watched from the comfort of the porch. The girls lived in

The site of the 2002 Christmas Eve murders, the renovated Wholaver house, now known as the "Lady Ann House," is one of the nicest on the block. Regardless, at the time of publication, it remains vacant, available for sale or rent. *Author's private collection.*

constant fear. In the molestation arrest report filed by Sergeant Richard Hiester Jr., he wrote, "Both are very fearful of their father and indicated that he is going to get them for telling." Jean Wholaver changed the locks, which made the girls feel a bit safer.

Fugitive recovery agents found Ernest Wholaver in Cambria County the following day at about 7:00 p.m. Although neighbors were certain of his guilt, police questioned and released Wholaver the same day without charges. Wholaver had denied involvement in the slayings. A week later, police implicated another Wholaver in the murders. Scott Wholaver, Ernest Wholaver's brother, found himself behind bars. Scott confessed to the police that he drove his older brother from Cambria County to Middletown in the early morning hours of Christmas Eve. The two had been drinking into the wee hours of the morning when Ernest told him that he needed a ride to Middletown to pick up his puppy. The two took turns driving a truck owned by the family business on the long, drunken ride from St. Benedict to Middletown. Before they reached Middletown, they stopped so Ernest could change into dark clothing.

Near dawn, Scott waited a block down the street while a gloved and masked Ernest Wholaver cut the telephone lines and then entered the house by reaching through a broken panel on the garage door to pull an emergency release cord, which allowed him to open the garage door manually. Once inside the garage, he was free to enter the house. He then gruesomely but meticulously made his way through the house, killing his wife and his two daughters. The district attorney believed that Scott Wholaver knew what his brother intended to do, but Scott claimed he did not. Ernest came back to the truck five to ten minutes later, excited and shaking, and told his brother to "drive, drive, drive."

Ernest told Scott, "You wouldn't believe what I saw." The two concocted a deer-hunting alibi, one that would put them far from Middletown on Christmas Eve. On the long ride back to St. Benedict, the pair stopped in Clearfield County for Ernest to change again and leave items in the woods, including a .22-caliber revolver. Although police accepted Scott's claim that he was not the triggerman and only the driver, they charged him with three counts of murder nonetheless. Ernest continued to maintain his innocence.

Scott Wholaver agreed to plead guilty to three counts of third-degree murder in exchange for testifying against his brother, which reduced the penalty from possible death to twelve to twenty-five years in state prison. The police were satisfied that Ernest had sufficient motive to kill his daughters, but Ernest's attorney, Spero Lappas, disagreed. He told the *Patriot-News*, "Scott is desperate and he's at the mercy of the powerful forces. The fact that Scott Wholaver testified against [Ernest] means nothing. Desperate and devious brothers have been harming one another since Cain slew Abel."

The district attorney charged Ernest with three counts of first-degree murder, burglary, conspiracy to commit burglary, obstruction of the administration of the law (for the false alibi) and reckless endangerment of another person (by killing her mother, Ernest left his nine-month-old granddaughter unattended for more than twenty-four hours).

The intrigue continued when, in addition to these charges, Ernest Wholaver was charged with criminal solicitation to commit murder. Wholaver attempted to hire a contract killer to murder Francisco

Ramos, the father of Victoria Wholaver's daughter Madison, as part of an elaborate scheme to frame the ex-boyfriend with the multiple murders. The hit man would make Francisco appear to have taken his own life and then plant a suicide note on his body confessing to the Wholaver family murders and clearing Ernest Wholaver's name. A jailhouse snitch informed authorities of Wholaver's plan early on, and police were able to document Wholaver's attempts to put out a contract on Francisco's life. The West Virginia hit man turned out to be an undercover Drug Enforcement Administration agent. The district attorney decided that there was enough evidence to seek the death penalty against Ernest Wholaver.

With Scott Wholaver as the prosecution's star witness, Ernest Wholaver was convicted and received three death sentences on August 31, 2004. He also received additional years for the other crimes. Wholaver's attorney appealed the case, but the Supreme Court of Pennsylvania ultimately upheld the death sentence in August 2006. Wholaver was set to be executed on June 20, 2006, but he received a stay of execution from the Dauphin County Court of Common Pleas. He is still on death row.

The Wholaver house sat vacant for six years, indelibly haunted. In contrast to the many other spectral locations in South Central Pennsylvania, the house is haunted by memories, not ghosts. In April 2008, at a Dauphin County sheriff's sale, Herbert Moore bought the property for $131,601, planning to renovate the house and rent it out. Sitting in mourning for those six long years without heat or air conditioning, the house had begun to deteriorate under the weight of its own melancholy. Moore demolished most of the house, leaving only the foundation. His intent was to rent to businessmen who would live in the house while looking for somewhere else to buy. The attractive yellow house sits on the corner of North Union and West Roosevelt, the lawn meticulously manicured. Despite its elegance, the five-bedroom, three-story colonial "Lady Anna House" sits empty, still haunted despite the renovation. A sign out front offers its availability "for rent or sale."

Part IV

GHOSTS, PHANTOMS AND UFOS

GHOSTS OF SWATARA

This is a particularly interesting section from a series that—judging by its title alone—would seem incapable of covering anything of interest: Notes and Queries, Historical and Genealogical, Chiefly Relating to Interior Pennsylvania. *Who would think that one note of interest in such a stodgy-sounding tome would be on the topic of ghosts? Even one hundred years ago, residents worried that ghosts were disappearing from the Pennsylvania landscape. At the very least, I hope my book proves that ghost stories are alive and well, as long as we know the right places to look.*

The superstitions of a past age are always interesting as well as instructive, for without a knowledge of them no just appreciation of the motives and actions of the people can be had.

We do not intend to present anything like a complete view of the superstitions which have been, and to some extent still are, prevalent in this vicinity, but shall confine ourselves to a brief and necessarily imperfect review of its *ghosts*, reserving for some future occasion a more interesting and more practical phase for the subject, the *Folk lore* of our ancestors. These worthies brought with them across the seas the prevailing superstitions of Europe, and as the population of every locality is composed of the descendants of various nationalities, we have here the commingling of the superstitions of the several countries, but principally of Great Britain and Germany. The Irish *Ben-Shie*, the Scottish *Wraith*, the English *Ghost*, and the German *Kobold*, all abounded and formed a heterogeneous congregation of shades, the like of which could not be found anywhere outside of America. This motley assembly probably gave rise to the provincialism *Spook*, which seems to have been applied to almost every unearthly sight or sound seen or heard at night. For the present we shall not trouble ourselves to make the nice distinction which exists between the ghostly fraternity of the different nations mentioned above, but be content with calling them all ghosts without inquiring from whence they are derived.

Forty-three years ago, when the vote was announced which carried the free school system in Swatara, the late Robert Wilson, of Highspire, prophesied that in twenty years there would not be a ghost in the township. This at the time seemed preposterous, for the hills of Swatara and the region around about were literally "fringed with ghosts." Yet the prophecy has been so substantially fulfilled that few of our people under forty years of age ever "saw a ghost"; and an old resident of Chambers' Hill, who, in his younger days, was very familiar with the "awful faces of other time," lately said in tones of sadness, "They are getting thin." The old man spoke as though the departure of the ghosts had deprived him of a part of his life, and left a void which it was now too late to fill; and doubtless his feelings were akin to those of the aged hunter whom civilization had overtaken, and with ruthless hand swept away the haunts' favorite game.

Three-quarters of a century ago ghosts were everywhere, although some localities were more prolific than others. Of these the region lying along Chambers' Hill, between Churchville and "Fiddler's Elbow," on the Swatara, was celebrated above its neighbors. And here, had we the time, we might stop to express our admiration of the great law of compensation which operates throughout the universe. What this region lacked in material resources, was abundantly made up in ghosts. At the time of which we write, and for many years after, this ridge was an unbroken forest, with a line of farms along its southern slope, and to this day the wild glens and steep hillsides near the Swatara present almost the same appearance as when the red hunter trod the forest in absolute ignorance of the existence of his pale-faced brothers.

Within the limits above described, are several of those small neglected graveyards, so common throughout our country, that even to-day, though in the midst of cultivated fields, are surrounded by an atmosphere which requires only a slight effort of the imagination to fill with phantoms and hobgoblins. These spots were surrounded by thick woods in the palmy days of ghosts, who held high carnival within their precincts. Many were the stories told of ghostly processions wending their way through the woods to visit friends in some neighboring yard, and one instance is related of a general muster of all the ghosts of Chamber's Hill and the country southward, to attend some great gathering held somewhere to the northward. The rendezvous was near the place where the church now stands, and those who witnessed it declared that when the ghosts took up the line of march, although they were four abreast, the head of the column had disappeared over the Paxtang hills before the rear had fallen into line. No one had the hardihood to follow and ascertain the place of meeting; nor has there come to us the slightest hint as to the business which called together this vast assemblage. The individual, upon whose authority our knowledge of this weird spectacle rests was an honest fellow of considerable experience in these matters, but such a timid mortal that he rarely remained upon the scene long enough to obtain full information as to the proceedings of the ghosts he encountered, almost invariably taking to his heels—and by this constant practice at the top of his speed he came to be remarkably fleet of foot. He once crossed the valley, followed by a ghost, in such an incredibly short space of time, that a number of gentlemen had the curiosity to go over the ground next morning and measure his steps—they found that he had cleared ten feet at every step. He has, himself, been a ghost these sixteen years or more.

Among the inmates of these quiet graveyards were certain wayward ghosts, who seemed to be at variant with their fellows and who wandered about solitary and alone, haunting old buildings and out-of-the-way "nooks and corners." They were usually harmless and only troublesome in so far as they occasionally frightened the belated wight who encountered them in their vagrant wanderings. There was another class of ghosts from which Chamber's Hill was singularly free—but who roamed not far away—the somber shades of suicides and murderers. These were such disagreeable and dangerous customers that it was not deemed prudent for either man or beast to cross their paths.

Of the multitude of ghosts which once traversed this region, but two remain. One of these is a staid and sober fellow, of prepossessing presence, who is the occupant of an unknown grave in a little cemetery in the fields south of the Chambers' road. He never leaves his accustomed beat, which leads from the cemetery across the fields to a ravine in the woods. After remaining here an hour or more (no one knows how engaged) he returns by the same route and as he nears the cemetery vanishes away. He always appears in his shirt sleeves and with no covering for his head save his thin gray hair, and can be seen any night about twelve o'clock by those from whose eyes the scales have fallen.

The second is that of a celebrated witch, who, in her day and generation, exerted considerable influence, but as a ghost she has never amounted to much and is now rarely seen. She appears in the shape of a large black dog with a chain around his neck and a body as long as a fence rail, with a tail to correspond—a very formidable appearance, from which the beholder always beats such a rapid retreat that no damage has yet resulted.

The third is an erratic ghost, and upon occasions disposed to be frolicsome. He has been known to several generations as "The Headless Wood-chopper," although he is not always cutting wood, nor does he always carry an axe. His origin is lost in antiquity, and it is doubtful whether he was ever the owner of a grave-yard. He seems to be master of his own movements, and comes and goes when and where he pleases, cuts wood or not as he feels disposed, and seems to delight in appearing at odd and unlooked for times and places. A volume might be filled with his exploits, but we have time and space for only one or two.

Less than ten years ago there was living in the valley an old gentleman, whose word in the ordinary affairs of life passed for truth, who used to relate in all sincerity, the story of an encounter he once had with "The Headless Wood-chopper." He had been below Middletown with his four-horse team, and was so late starting home that night overtook him before he reached "Fiddler's Elbow," between which point and the turnpike road, a distance of probably a mile and a quarter, the road lay through a dark and lonely wood. He had scarcely left the "elbow" when his horses affrighted at something which in the darkness he could not see. He succeeded in holding his horses in check, but could not quiet them.

As his eyes became more accustomed to the darkness, he observed what seemed to him a short man walking beside his team on the right side of the road, who in a few moments sprang upon the back of the off-wheel horse, a gray beast which enabled the gentleman to observe accurately the outlines of the figure upon his back. They rode thus close together until they approached the edge of the timber, when the apparition sprang to the ground on all fours and ran away like a dog. During this long ride the gentleman had ample time to scan the short man most closely, and that he was the "Headless Wood-chopper," there was in his mind no doubt. What convinced him that no deception had been practiced upon him was the fact that when he reached home, although it was a cold night, his horses were in a "lather of sweat and trembling like leaves," and continued in that state until toward morning. (That there were spirits of some kind in the woods that night seems not improbable.)

The last appearance of this celebrated ghost was within the present year, near the house of an aged couple living some miles west of the scene of the adventure related above. It was a bright moonlight night. A friend had spent the evening with some old folks, listening to the many stories of ghosts, witches and "sic like cattle," with which the old man's mind is richly stored. He had taken his departure, and had reached the middle of the road in front of the house not a dozen steps from the door, when he became conscious of something near him. He looked over his left shoulder and beheld a ghost capering as if in high glee. His fright was so great that he reached the door at almost a single bound, and entered speechless. The old man, upon looking out to ascertain the cause, recognized the "Headless Wood-chopper," who always went unencumbered, or at most with nothing but his axe, and as he has not been seen since, it is believed that the term of his ghostly service expired on that very night, and that he was departing in joyous mood for some other and nobler sphere of action.

COOKING UP SPOOKS

In Hummelstown, fast asleep in the middle of the night, the Seibert family awoke to the sound of footsteps and cabinet doors opening and closing. They hurried downstairs, but as always, the kitchen was empty—empty except for familiar, pleasant aromas. They smelled bacon, coffee, chocolate cake, sausage and sugar cookies. Mr. and Mrs. Seibert often smell coffee in the morning and assume that the other has risen and started the pot when they are, in fact, still asleep next to each other. The Seiberts, at first concerned they were either losing their minds or experiencing the early symptoms of a stroke, came to the conclusion that they were hosting a ghostly houseguest. And they think that they have even figured out the ghost's worldly identity. Their neighbor Margaret's parents lived their entire married lives in the house. When they mentioned the haunting to her, Margaret did not take offense, nor was she shocked. She simply told them that the ghost must be her mother, who was known to love to cook. Ever since then, the Seiberts have enjoyed hosting the benign spirit.

THE LOST HUNTER

In 1952, a group of men set out for a day of hunting on Shade Mountain near Dry Gap. It was a foggy day. This was the first hunt for one young boy in the group. The men told him to stay close to a few old-timers who knew the area well. They put the boy at a good deer crossing and told him to stay there until they returned. The boy sat patiently waiting for a deer. Soon enough, one walked right by him. He aimed and fired. His shot was true, and the deer stumbled and then ran. The boy followed the blood trail for a long time but ultimately gave up. It was only then that he realized how lost he was. He walked and walked and walked some more, but he couldn't find any of the other hunters.

When the other men returned and found the boy missing, they organized a massive search, but the boy had disappeared. To this day, his body has never been found. A few years ago, a hunter in Dry Gap walked into a fog bank. While he was stumbling through the fog, he ran across a small boy sitting by a fire. The boy said that he was lost, so the man told him to follow him, and he would lead him out of the fog. The man finally found a clearing, but when he turned around to tell the boy that he knew the way out from there, the boy was gone. He told his hunting buddy about the lost boy in the odd, vintage hunting gear. The other hunter recognized the description and told the man that he had just met the Lost Hunter of Shade Mountain. Hunters today say that if you walk into a fog bank in the Dry Gap, you just may meet the lost boy, too.

LUCY PRETTY EAGLE

Lucy Pretty Eagle haunts the Coren Apartments at the Carlisle Barracks, formerly the Carlisle Indian School. Lucy attended the Carlisle Indian School and died there at the tender age of eighteen. She may have been

Lucy Pretty Eagle's gravestone, decorated with violets at the Carlisle Indian School. *Courtesy of the Archives of Pennsylvania Folklife and Ethnography.*

buried alive while in an altered state of consciousness or suffering from some other illness. She is buried in Section C, Plot 21 of the Indian School Cemetery, on the eastern edge of the Carlisle Barracks. Her headstone reads March 9, 1884. Flowers almost always decorate Lucy's grave, but no one knows who places them there. A history teacher at Wilson Middle School takes his class to the cemetery every year as part of a school field trip, and every year since 1963, flowers have adorned Lucy's grave. Lucy now allegedly haunts the Coren Apartments. She has been heard cooking in the kitchen and moving around in small crawl spaces. One of the current residents, a major skeptic, said that Lucy is nothing more than an annoying rattling of the heat pipes, one that makes it difficult to keep a decent babysitter. A former resident of the apartment told of a houseguest who had ridiculed the ghost stories of Lucy Pretty Eagle. Later that evening, when the guest went to relieve himself, he found himself locked in the bathroom.

Man in the Attic

In Bunkertown today, there is an old, run-down house. During the Great Depression of the 1930s, this house was one of the stateliest in Bunkertown. The owner was very rich, and he didn't mind showing it off. The Depression forced the once wealthy gentleman to declare bankruptcy. Afterward, he spiraled into a depression and then one day disappeared without a trace. The town searched for the man, but he couldn't be found. A week after the search concluded, a young girl passing the house detected a terrible odor. She reported the smell to her father, who reported it to the police. The police searched the house again and this time found a secret passageway that led to the attic. In the attic, they found the man hanging above a knocked-over chair, beginning to decay. After police found the corpse, no one wanted anything to do with the house, and it remained empty. A year later, a young man walking his dog past the house glanced over and saw a man staring out of the attic window. He called to the man but received no reply—just a cold stare. Knowing that the house was supposed to be vacant, the curious boy and his dog investigated, entering the house and climbing to the attic, but they found no one. Since then, other residents of Bunkertown have reported a man staring at them out of the attic window, but upon closer inspection, the attic is always found to be vacant.

Specter of the Spurned Spouse

There's a house in Greencastle close to the Macedonia United Brethren Church, out in the country near the Maryland line. A retired army officer bought the house and moved in with his wife and his two little girls. They soon began to feel an unsettling presence in the house. They all sensed it, but at first no one said a word. They didn't want the others to think them crazy. But the unsettling feeling didn't stop. They often felt like someone was watching them. Even when they were alone, they felt like the house wasn't truly empty. Pushed to the brink, the husband and wife sat down and told each other what they had felt. Just hearing that they were not experiencing this alone relieved some of the stress.

The couple decided to research the history of the house. They found that a married couple had lived in the house for a long time before them. The wife, however, died a very mysterious and untimely death. Suspicious police investigated but could not prove foul play. The investigation stalled, and the case was ultimately dropped. The officer's wife decided to track down the husband. Once she discovered the widower's whereabouts, she walked around the house shouting, "He doesn't live here anymore! He doesn't live here anymore!" Over and over again, "He doesn't live here anymore!" Then she shouted his new address, and the ghost went away.

Tale of the Union Soldier

At the onset of the Civil War, a young couple had married as trouble brewed between the North and the South. The South seceded from the Union, and the country was at war. The young man felt duty bound to serve his country. He kissed his bride goodbye and told her that he would return as soon as the war was won. The first few months were manageable because the wife received a letter from her husband every week. But then one week the letters stopped, and the wife knew that her husband was dead. Several weeks after the letters had stopped, the woman heard fighting in the distance. She knew that this day would come, but she had hoped that her husband would be home to protect her.

When the cannons and gunfire stopped, she heard a knock at her front door. She picked up the gun that her husband had left her, loaded it and told the visitor that the door was open. As the door creaked open, a fearsome soldier with long, unkempt hair and a dirty gray uniform walked in, sending a surge of fear straight into her stomach. Knowing that he had only one thing on his mind, the good wife pulled the trigger, and the soldier fell dead. She went to the soldier, rolling him over to see his face. Looking into his eyes, she recognized the man. It was her beloved husband, returned from the war, his uniform covered in dust.

Legend has it that on those cool nights in the summer when there is a little mist in the mountains, campers can hear the Union soldier walking through the woods, making his way back to his sweetheart.

THE BARBER'S GHOST

The tale of the Barber's Ghost, found in the 1866 edition of Baer's Agriculture Almanac, *is an excellent example of the many possibilities of the legend genre. What begins as a supernatural haunted tavern legend can soon turn into a joke. Many variants of this humorous legend exist, some focusing more on the supernatural aspect than others, but this version is my favorite.*

A gentleman, traveling some years since in the upper part of this state called a tavern and requested entertainment for the night. The landlord informed him that it was out of his power to accommodate him, as his house was already full. He persisted in stopping, as he, as well as his horse, were almost exhausted with traveling. After much solicitation, the landlord consented to his stopping, provided he would sleep in a certain room that had not been occupied for a long time, in consequence of the belief that it was haunted by the ghost of a barber, who was reported to have been murdered in that room some years before.

"Very well" says the man, "I'm not afraid of ghosts."

After having refreshed himself, he inquired of the landlord how and in what manner the room in which he was to lodge was haunted. The landlord replied that shortly after they retired to rest an unknown voice was heard, in a trembling and protracted accent, "Do you want to be shaved?"

"Well," replied the man, "if he comes he may shave me."

He then requested to be shown to the apartment, in going to which he was conducted through a large room where were seated a great number of persons at a gambling table. Feeling a curiosity which almost every one possesses after having heard ghost stories, he carefully searched every corner of his room, but could discover nothing but the usual furniture of the apartment. He then lay down, but did not close his eyes to sleep immediately; and in a few minutes he imagined he heard a voice saying, "Do you w-a-n-t to be s-h-a-v-e-d?"

He arose from his bed and searched every part of the room, but could discover nothing. He again went to bed; but no sooner had he began to compose himself to sleep, than the question was again repeated. He again arose and went to the window, the sound appearing to proceed from that quarter, he again heard the sound distinctly; and convinced that it was from without, he opened the window, when the question was repeated full in his ear, which startled him not a little. Upon a minute examination, however, he observed that the limb of a large oak tree, which stood under the window, projected so near the house that every breath of wind, to a lively imagination, made a noise resembling the interrogation, "Do you w-a-n-t to be s-h-a-v-e-d?"

Having satisfied himself that his ghost was nothing more nor less than the limb of a tree coming in contact with the house, he again went to bed, and attempted to get asleep; he was now interrupted by peals of laughter, and an occasional volley of oaths and curses, from the room where the gamblers were assembled. Thinking that he could turn the late discovery to his own advantage, he took a sheet from the bed and wrapped it around him, and taking the wash-basin in his hand, and throwing the towel over his arm, proceeded to the room of the gamblers, and suddenly opening the door, walked in, exclaiming in a tremulous voice, "Do you w-a-n-t to be s-h-a-v-e-d?"

Terrified at the sudden appearance of the ghost, the gamblers were thrown into the greatest confusion in attempting to escape it—some jumping through the windows, and others tumbling head over heels down stairs. Our ghost, taking advantage of the clear room, deliberately swept a large amount of the money from the table into the basin and retired unseen to his own room.

The next morning he found the house in the utmost confusion. He was immediately asked if he rested well, to which he replied in the affirmative.

"Well, no wonder," said the landlord, "for the ghost, instead of going to his own room, made a mistake, and came to ours, frightened us out of the room and took away every dollar of our money."

The guest, without being the least suspected, quietly ate his own breakfast, and departed, many hundred dollars the richer by the adventure.

SUMMER OF THE UFO

South Central Pennsylvania saw a rash of UFO sightings between 1967 and 1968. Pennsylvanians set up impromptu viewing parties on rural back roads and overwhelmed local newspapers with daily reports. The sightings were so numerous and the phenomenon so widespread that both local police departments and the National Investigations Committee on Aerial Phenomena chose to investigate. The local affiliate of NICAP conducted a detailed study of reported sightings. By early June, it had concluded that at least thirty sightings were "genuine."

Three children and an adult reported one of the most exciting sightings on April 1, 1967, toward the beginning of the UFO timeframe, before the sightings came flooding in. Playing outside their homes on Linglestown Road, three children watched a large, round object descend close to the ground, about two hundred feet from them. The object emitted no noise and alternated between colors. Its primary interest seemed to be the nearby power lines. For two minutes, it shot a ray of light that landed on the power lines. As the UFO ascended back into the evening sky and the alarmed children ran for safety, a neighbor stepping out of his house watched the UFO fly off with a "jet trail in its wake."

Two months later, among a mounting deluge of "genuine" sightings, a couple driving near the DeHart Dam in Middle Paxton Township reported sighting an alien rather than a UFO. What first appeared to be a deer—a common sight in late spring in Central Pennsylvania—turned into a "strange person with glowing eyes" as they got closer. On the same night and only four miles away, an unnerved dog woke its owners. As they went to calm their canine, the man and woman spotted "a huge white light and heard a droning noise," as well as "high-pitched, unintelligible language." The couple alerted local authorities, but alas, all signs of UFO activity had vanished by the time the police arrived.

In the coming day and months, sightings poured in from all over South Central Pennsylvania. Pennsylvanians were no longer haphazardly stumbling upon UFOs; they were actively seeking them out. The daily newspaper articles, pleasant summer nights and possibility of seeing a real UFO led to crowds of nightly spectators mingling on Pennsylvania's elevated, rural back roads, studying the night sky for signs of extraterrestrial life. The crowds were so large and so lively that some vendors even set up shop. Many of the summer's reports came from this crowd, and some were obvious misinterpretations: planets, shooting stars and aircraft, in addition to the occasional hoax.

On the other hand, observers reported an incredible number of genuine, tenable sightings. Tower Road (named for its numerous radio and television towers), in East Pennsboro Township and Brandy Lane near the Naval Supply Depot in Mechanicsburg, hosted two of these nightly gatherings. In late June, a large crowd on Brandy Lane spotted a "white, glowing light with two smaller reddish-orange lights" moving west to east, parallel with the road. They quickly accelerated and shot out of view. The proximity of the Naval Supply Depot to Brady Lane provided an explanation for the UFO's motives. The UFO was hovering to check on the mysterious mounds near the fence in the corner of the base rumored to be anything from corpses to nuclear waste (they're surpluses of iron ore).

By July 1967, Edward Condon and his University of Colorado UFO Project—sponsored by the United States Air Force and sometimes informally called the Condon Committee—had arrived in South Central Pennsylvania to conduct UFO research. Working with local authorities, witnesses and NICAP, the committee concluded that there was sufficient evidence to warrant a full investigation. Placing an all-sky surveillance camera on top of Front Street's Harrisburg Hospital, one of the tallest buildings in the city at the time, the Colorado UFO Project monitored the Dauphin County skies for seventeen nights. The camera took close to ten thousand pictures in this time but came away with no smoking gun. The committee listed twelve of the images as "questionable." The project concluded, "Even though scores of UFOs were reported during that time, that the investigator could find nothing to examine with his instruments and nothing remarkable on thousands of all-sky camera exposures with the exceptions noted above is highly significant."

The Condon Committee's report actually led to more questions than answers. Why could the all-sky camera only capture twelve questionable images in seventeen days when people in the rest of the state were seeing as many sightings per day? Why were copies of those twelve questionable images never released to the public? Was the committee more interested in covering up the Pennsylvania phenomenon than investigating it? Critics have heaped scorn on Edward Condon and his government-funded project. Stanton Friedman pointed out:

When his unscientific attitude could no longer be ignored, two scientist members of the Colorado group went public with a damaging document and were promptly fired. Despite the open controversy, the final report of the Condon Committee was completed in 1968, blessed by the National Academy of Sciences, and then published commercially. Dr. Condon's thoroughly negative summation was in stark contrast to the fascinating data buried in the lengthy report, where 30 percent of the cases were left without conventional explanation. Of more than 550 unexplained reports then in the Project Blue Book Files, only three were considered by the University of Colorado, while current sightings having little chance of being significant were given expensive on-the-spot investigations.

UFO investigators have continued to shower Edward Condon with disdain, finding him complicit in a government-funded coverup. By fall, the daily reports had begun to cool. NICAP and the Civil Air Patrol joined forces in an effort to seek out UFOs, but the summer of 1967 would prove to have been the apex of the event.

Although there would never be a summer like 1967 again, reports of UFO sightings in South Central Pennsylvania have continued to roll in ever since. In 2008, a *Patriot-News* reporter caught a small green saucer flying over Dillsburg. On June 27, 2012, just before midnight, Millersville University mathematics professor Noel Heitmann reported seeing a "neon-green light flashing through the sky" while traveling the Pennsylvania Turnpike about fifteen miles west of Harrisburg. The light "stretched from on end of the horizon to the other" before "the brilliance morphed into the shape of a silo" and disappeared. Another man contacted the *Patriot-News* reporting a similar phenomenon around the same time. Harrisburg International Airport is in the vicinity, and representatives claim that they have received similar inquiries before, but they are not able to explain them.

THE WHITE LADY

The legend most frequently told in the Altoona area concerns the White Lady, or the Lady in the White Dress. A young man and woman in their late teens or early twenties were in love and wanted to marry, but none of the parents consented to the marriage. Because of this, on a cool and rainy night in the early 1960s, the two decided to run off and elope. The lovers' journey away from home brought them to Buckhorn Mountain and a steep and winding road that is known to cause frequent accidents. Traveling down the mountain on the dark and foggy night, they lost control of the car and careened over the side to their deaths in the valley below. After the crash, the authorities recovered the boy's body, but the girl's was never found. The girl now haunts the mountain on dark and rainy nights, wearing the wedding dress that she never had the chance to wear.

The legend is especially popular among teenagers, whether on camping trips or at outdoor drinking parties held in the woods. The legend often comes up in conversation during double dates at the Wopsononock lookout, close to Buckhorn Mountain. Boys take girls to an old, abandoned house in the woods where the White Lady is supposed to live and try to convince them to explore the house with them. The girls are rarely persuaded.

Sixty-year Altoona resident Dot grew up a stone's throw away from Buckhorn Mountain and knows the legend well. Her version, however, is quite different. Hers is set one hundred years earlier, in the 1860s. Two young lovers were rushing off into the night to elope. They traveled down Buckhorn Mountain, and in their haste, their horse and buggy overturned, throwing both of them over the side. The fatal crash killed both lovers, and the only thing that remained was the white wedding dress, torn from its box, on the side of the road. Now the girl returns to Buckhorn Mountain every twenty years on foggy nights and walks the road in the white wedding dress that she never got to wear. Dot recalled learning about the legend as a teenager from the neighborhood kids who were a few years older. Most of the time, the story would come up on dark, foggy nights or when there was a fatal accident on the mountain.

Resident Danielle's version also takes place during the Civil War, although it is otherwise quite different. During the Civil War, a newlywed couple traveled through Altoona on the way to their honeymoon. Locals found out about the couple and were outraged to hear that Southerners were in their area. As the newlyweds navigated the Wopsononock Mountain, locals forced their carriage off the side of the road. They pulled the bride from the carriage and hanged her from a nearby tree. After making the groom watch, he was shot and killed. Ever since, the bride walks up and down the Wopsononock Mountain every night, looking for her husband.

Residents also report meeting the White Lady at the bottom of Buckhorn Mountain, where she asks for a ride. She does not talk at all during the ascent, except to say that she would like to be dropped off at the top of the mountain. At the top, near a local bar called the Buckhorn Inn, the driver looks over to ask if this is spot, only to find that the woman has disappeared. (This version of the legend shares much in common with the nationally known "Vanishing Hitchhiker" legend.) Dot believes that one function of the legend is an entertaining way to remind us how dangerous the mountain can be, especially on foggy nights.

Donna has lived at the bottom of Buckhorn Mountain all of her life. She grew up with yet another version of the legend. In the 1940s, a newlywed couple on their wedding night traveled along Skyline Drive, a two-mile stretch of road that connects the Buckhorn and the Wopsononock Mountains. When the couple came to the edge of Skyline Drive, they mistakenly took a left instead of a right. This one mistake, combined with the dense fog and rain, sent the couple plunging off the edge of the Wopsononock lookout, killing them both instantly. Now, on nights similar to that one, the girl supposedly wanders the Wopsononock lookout and Skyline Drive in her white wedding dress. All couples are advised not to go to the lookout on foggy and rainy nights for fear of the White Lady.

Steve collected another version. Hundreds of years ago, a newly married couple traveled the Wopsononock Mountain. The carriage suddenly jolted, and the couple were thrown from their seats. The wife survived, but the husband plummeted over the side of the mountain and was never found. People now report seeing the woman in her white dress, dragging an empty casket behind her, still looking for her beloved husband so she can give him a proper burial.

Newer versions show the harm the White Lady can cause to those who don't heed the warnings. A few years back, a group of teenagers went to the foot of the Wopsononock Mountain in search of the White Lady. One of the teenagers was a star football payer. He spotted the lady and attempted to tackle her but came up empty. The ghost whispered in his ear, "You'll never play football again." That week in practice, he broke his leg in three places, ending his season.

HALL'S TOWER

On a nearly hidden side road in Mechanicsburg, deep in a field, sits a burned-out, sixteen-story tower so unusual that it is eerie even without a background legend. The tower, which can be seen from a distance,

The unnerving Hall's Tower, seen standing alone in a field in Mechanicsburg. *Author's private collection.*

was originally part of a mansion built by the eccentric John Hall. The tower was never completed but was meant to hold Swiss bells. The house sits next to the tower and looks tiny by comparison. The property also included a moat and a squash court. John Hall built his dream home with money he embezzled from his father. He did jail time and went bankrupt.

Numerous legends circulate about the history of the property. Some claim that John Hall himself set the property on fire. Whether the house was burned empty or with his family inside varies from teller to teller. The entire Hall clan is, in fact, still alive, and one son may still live in the guesthouse, although his father no longer owns the property. Adding to the legend, a diver hired to drain the swamp drowned after being caught in the drainpipe. Later, the vacant property became a happening party location for local teenagers. One of these teenagers, Ernie Barr, fell to his death climbing the tower. His friends claim that he was intoxicated, but others claim that the ghost may have pushed Ernie to his death. While this used to be an automobile legend, the road has recently been chained off, making the road inaccessible to vehicles.

Part V
HILLS, HOUSES AND HOLLOWS

DEVIL'S FORGE

One excellent, oft-overlooked source of local legendry is the county history. Without any strict rules to follow and full of stories of all sorts, local legends often found their way into these volumes. In addition, rampant, routine partial plagiarism of such materials from text to text in the nineteenth and early twentieth centuries gave the materials a folkloric quality even in print. This particular legend comes from The History of Perry County.

The "old forge" with the legend variously told (the following in the substance of the various versions) of the Devil's Hole, about a mile distant, gave our daily cow-hunts an interest, and oftimes a dread that will not soon be forgotten.

The legend of Forge Hill has sufficient local interest to claim the following recital: Before Lewis's forge was in operation, it is related that the devil contracted with three men to prepare him an underground dwelling, and secure him a black sheep, without a white spot on it, until he should come to examine them. A specified time was agreed upon for the completion of this subterranean abode, for which, and the sheep, the builders were to receive a half-bushel of silver dollars. The work was completed, the sheep secured, and the laborers awaited the coming of his satanic majesty. Precisely at the appointed time the devil appeared in the air. Showing his cloven foot, to the no little discomfort of the builders, as he alighted at the open door of his intended abode. He proceeded to an examination of the building which was constructed underground of logs, and covered with earth, so that it might appear at the surface nothing more than a elevation of the summit of a hill, requiring a *sesame* to open it. The abode was pronounced satisfactory; when the sheep was produced with the greatest confidence that it was black enough to satisfy the requirements. Imagine their utter astonishment when the devil no sooner saw the sheep than he demanded one of them, declaring that it was not without a white spot, as agreed upon, and in order to convince the contractors that such was the case he lifted it from its feet and turned it upon its back, when, lo, the white spot was there. This so alarmed one of the men, who was a [Pennsylvania] Dutchman, that he began to cry out: "Heilig Yasu! Heilig Yasu!" whereupon his insulted devilship departed, taking with him the half bushel of money, leaving the chagrined builders in a bewildered condition, one of who it is said remained insane during the rest of his life.

This is briefly the legend which has been handed down from parents to children, and firmly believed. It probably had no better foundation in fact than that this so-called *Devil's Hole* was a robbers' cave.

AGATHA BAKER AND THE BAKER MANSION

The motif of a young lady and a white wedding dress is also present in the legend of Agatha Baker and the Baker Mansion, which is located in Altoona, Pennsylvania. Daughter of owner and millionaire Elias Baker, Agatha Baker haunts the Baker Mansion. In her twenties, Agatha Baker fell in love with one of her father's young ironworkers, but Elias Baker would not permit his daughter to marry the poor young man. Agatha vowed that if she could not marry her love, she would never marry—and she never did. In 1941, the Blair County Historical Society turned the Baker Mansion into a museum for the display of old rugs, guns, books and furniture. In Agatha's winter room, an airtight glass case holds a white wedding dress from the 1830s. Even though the wedding dress is in an airtight case, the dress changes positions from time to time. A pair of slippers in a separate case pull the same trick. Mansion staff members claim to have seen the wedding dress dance to music playing downstairs. Agatha Baker haunts the wedding dress, eternally envious of others enjoying the wedding she never had.

BURLINGTON FARM

The eighteenth-century Burlington Farm in Shippensburg sits on one hundred acres a mile and a half south of King Street on the Old Baltimore Road, out of view of the main road. Now abandoned, the brothers of Phi Sigma Kappa who lived there for several decades hosted a ghost they nicknamed "Garfield." The main house was a two-story, limestone Georgian residence with ten rooms, two bathrooms, a large living area, two kitchens and eight residents. More brothers lived outside the main house in the servants' house and an adjacent trailer. Long ago, it was also home to the first governor of Pennsylvania, Thomas Mifflin.

Yet another victim of the Civil War haunts the house. During the Civil War, Confederate soldiers occupied the house while fighting nearby. One Confederate soldier, fearing for his life and too frightened to fight, hid in the basement. Ironically, he froze to death in the basement, and his ghost now haunts the Burlington Farm. Not knowing his real name, the fraternity brothers nicknamed him "Garfield."

From the day they moved into the house in 1977, the fraternity brothers maintained that the house was haunted, a fact that was particularly noticeable when alone. The brothers would wake to footsteps in the attic, too heavy to be squirrels or rats. In a bedroom with a passageway to the attic, household dogs bark and growl for no apparent reason, their hair standing on end.

Turning the faucet off in the upstairs bathrooms, brothers would hear the water begin to flow again as soon as they left the bathroom. Similarly, objects moved from place to place with no explanation. Another brother claimed twice to have been woken at about 4:00 a.m. by short, high-pitched cackles emanating inches away from his face, frightening him badly and covering his body in goose bumps. Turning the light on, he found the room empty both times.

The Burlington Farm main house on a winter's day, circa 1985. *Courtesy of the Archives of Pennsylvania Folklife and Ethnography.*

Some claim to have seen Garfield, while many more have heard voices in the night. Although he supposedly died in the basement, there is general agreement that he now lives in the attic. A brother living in the servants' house swore that he heard voices crying out from the main house attic while he was the only one on the property. Later, he heard the dogs' excited barking in the main house. Knowing that no one was home, he entered the house to check on them. Once again, he found the dogs standing at the bottom of the steps to the attic, staring upstairs and growling.

CHESAPEAKE NAIL WORKS

The Chesapeake Nail Works was built in 1866 on Dock Street. The clock from the 1878 nail works explosion has become a celebrity in its own right. On the top of the clock reads the words, "No tick here." The clock hung in the Chesapeake Nail Works, a plate mill in Harrisburg. In the

The Chesapeake Nail
Works clock, stopped
forever at 3:36. Above
the clock are written the
words "No tick here."
*Courtesy of Historical Society
of Dauphin County.*

early hours of June 25, 1878, a huge explosion rocked the mill. The clock
rested in a prominent position in the mill, and during the explosion, a
hard projectile dashed the clock, fracturing the face and marking for all
time the deadly moment that otherwise passed so quickly. Since 1878, the
clock has read 3:36, the precise time of the explosion.

The clock has become a curiosity among Pennsylvanians, a rare,
tangible embodiment of a horrific accident. Crowds have flocked to see
the clock, awed by its symbolic representation of the moment of death.
One person even offered a large sum to add it to her private collection,
but the Chesapeake Nail Works clock is not for sale. Although the

explosion came in the middle of the night, it claimed several lives. The explosion instantly killed Chambers Bowermaster, the boiler tender. Two others, John Hetrick and John Hess, both puddlers, succumbed to their wounds the following day. The three men were well liked and left behind grieving families. The other men of the mill, seeing the excitement that the clock provoked in the general public, photographed the clock and sold the prints, giving the proceeds to the affected families.

Gordon Nagle Trail

On Gordon Nagle Trail, three men raped and murdered a woman. One of them was her boyfriend, and the other two were his friends. All three had been drinking all day. One of the boyfriend's friends returned to the trail with another girl. While on the trail, he had car trouble and had to walk down the road looking for help. When he came back with a tow truck, the girl was gone. When he couldn't find her anywhere, he enlisted his other two friends to help him look for her. While they were looking for her, the boyfriend fell down a mineshaft and broke his neck, although he didn't have the luxury of an instant death. The man whose female friend was missing just wandered off and was never seen again. The last man is the one the murdered girl's spirit is still looking for. Ever since then, men are not supposed to travel on the Gordon Nagle Trail after midnight because the ghost of the girl is still looking for revenge. After midnight, car trouble on Gordon Nagle Trail is likely, and it may be the ghost of Gordon Nagle Trail trying to lure the third man into the woods.

House on Cider Press Road

Neglected for more than half a century, the house on Cider Press Road in Lower Paxton Township is old and abandoned. A legend trip to the house has become a rite of passage for the teenagers from the three high schools located near the house. The mystique of the house and its barn come from a widely known story. More than seventy years ago, a mother, a father and their two children lived in the house. The mother took the father and both of her children out to the barn across the street from the house. In the barn, she picked up an axe and killed her husband. She then turned on her own two children. Finally, she calmly crossed the street, returning to her own house, where she climbed to the third-floor attic and placed a shotgun in her mouth. Passersby can now see a blue light emanating from the attic. Legend tellers attribute the eerie light to the mother's spirit, watching all those who enter her domain. (The motif of a blue light can be found in legends throughout the United States.)

At more than ninety years old, Frank Kocevar bought the house and the adjacent forty acres in 1948. The Kocevar clan lives a block from the legendary house, where they enjoy a clear and unobstructed view. The family has kept a close watch over the property ever since their barn was set ablaze ten years ago. The family chases and threatens trespassers, especially on Halloween. All of this, of course, only adds to the mystique of the property. The house is often surrounded by fog, even on an otherwise clear day. Legend trippers are as enthusiastic about the house on Cider Press Road in winter as they are in the summer. Winters added the opportunity to check the snow for footprints, to see if anyone actually lived in the house. According to a family friend of the Kocevars, "Nothing ever happened in that house; the Kocevars would never have bought the house if any had." At least, that's what the Kocevars want the teens in the area to believe.

House on Spangler's Spring

In July 1863, the North and South clashed in the three-day battle at Gettysburg, now regarded as one of the bloodiest and most crucial engagements in American history. Ever since, legends of ghosts and spirits haunt Gettysburg. Lifelong Gettysburg resident Tom recalled the haunted house located near Spangler's Spring as the most authentic and frightening Gettysburg legend from his childhood. During the Battle of Gettysburg, the African American Dokes family lived in the house on

Spangler's Spring. When the Confederates took the house by force, they beheaded one of the sons as a means of striking fear into the hearts of Northern blacks.

Legend has it that every morning before dawn, the elderly mother hobbles outside with her lantern, calling the name of her dead son. The tale being widely circulated in the Gettysburg area, children were terrified of the possibility of running into the headless boy or the wrinkled old woman. Schoolmates circulated the legend among themselves, sometimes sitting together at night on the dark battlefield and telling ghost stories while teenagers dared one another to enter the house. This is the only real Gettysburg legend that Tom could remember as a child, and it scared him so severely that it stuck with him into adulthood.

LOST CHILDREN OF THE ALLEGHENIES

In 1856, Samuel Cox, his wife, Susannah, and their two young sons, seven-year-old George and five-year-old Joseph, settled in Lovely, a small town in Lincoln Township, after living for a time in Indiana. While in Indiana, the family had contracted malaria, but they quickly convalesced in Pennsylvania's cool mountain air. On an April morning, while sitting for breakfast, the family heard their dog, Spot, barking, signaling a treed squirrel. Samuel took his rifle from over the mantel and went to get meat for supper. Susannah busied herself with household chores, assuming that the boys had followed their father on the hunt. When Samuel returned an hour and a half later alone, the couple realized that the boys must have wandered off on their own. A party of more than one thousand searched for the boys for fourteen days and nights, but the boys remained missing.

During this time, Jacob and Sarah Dibert lived in Claysburg. Jacob did not know the mountains, but his wife's family lived in Pavia, a small town about ten miles from the Cox cabin. They knew the mountains well. The Diberts arrived early at church that Sunday to hear if there was any news on the missing Cox boys, only to find that they were still missing. During the service, the minister asked God to show how these boys might be found, to which Jacob said, "Amen." Not knowing the mountains, Jacob knew that he would not be much help looking for the children, but that night Jacob had a dream.

Jacob dreamed that he was alone in the woods, searching for the children. In his dream, he stepped on a fallen tree, and lying before the tree, he found a dead deer. Jacob jumped over the dead deer and continued down the trail, where he found a child's shoe. He used a fallen beech tree to cross a stream, navigated a ridge and entered a ravine. Next to a small stream trickling through the ravine, he found two boys lying dead whom he'd never seen before. Jacob told his wife about the dream but otherwise kept it to himself. The next night, he had the same dream. Jacob decided to tell his wife's brother, Harrison Whysong, who knew the mountains well.

Harrison was skeptical, but since he knew the ridge, the ravine and the stream, he agreed to take a look. On May 8, 1856, Harrison and Jacob stepped over a fallen tree, leaped over a dead deer, passed a child's shoe, crossed a stream on a fallen beech tree, went over a ridge and found the two boys lying next to the stream, dead.

Lover's Rock

Most Millersburgers are familiar with the legend of Lover's Rock. The rock rests on top of Berry's Mountain, south of the town. Some time between 1750 and 1800, two young English brothers crossed the mountain gap near town over the Old Indian Trail. There they found a band of Indians camped, journeying eastward to an Indian village at the end of the valley. While talking with the chief, they heard a young lady in a nearby teepee singing in English. Her song told them that the tribe had captured her and would make her marry an Indian prince. She begged them to help her, and they agreed. An hour later, they returned outside of her teepee, revealing their plan to her. The boys positioned two ponies near to camp. When the girl begged the chief for some time alone to pray to her god, she snuck into the bushes where the boys were hiding and escaped on horseback with one of the brothers. The other brother took off in another direction, deceiving the Indians by rolling a blanket up to look like a hidden girl. The Indians followed the wrong brother, wounding and catching him.

When the Indians questioned the wounded brother, he told them that the girl had been fatally injured falling from the pony, and he had hidden her behind Lover's Rock. He showed them the rock, and when the girl wasn't there, they searched the nearby bushes. As the sun set, the wounded brother climbed on top of Lover's Rock to see the sun set for one last time. As the sun sunk below the horizon, he drew his last breath and fell dead.

The Indians searched until dark, finding nothing. When they returned and found the young man's body lying next to the rock, they realized that they had been fooled once again. The next day, a company of soldiers from Fort Halifax searched for the brother. They found him at the base of Lover's Rock, buried beneath a pile of branches. While the rescue party was gathering up the corpse, a lone Indian appeared, the Indian prince who had been promised the captive girl and who now believed she was dead. For years, he searched for her body, which he never found. Now, on certain nights, the lone Indian appears, still searching for his promised bride. Little does he know that she escaped to safety at Fort Halifax and married her rescuer.

Loverock

Lykens is home to a legend similar to the Lover's Rock, locally known simply as Loverock, an immense formation of solid rock nestled in the side of the mountain. An Indian reservation once sat on the top of these cliffs. These Indians carved steps out of the mountain that lead down to seats on the front of the cliff used for lookout towers. One day, a band of Indian braves came to town thirsty for "firewater." Lykens enjoyed a friendly relationship with the tribe, and they were always welcome in town. But this day, the Indians became so intoxicated that on the way home, they abducted a young white girl and took her to their village. They bound her hands and feet and imprisoned her in a teepee on the outskirts of the camp.

A young brave who saw the drunken party bring the girl into the village went to the chief and asked if he could bring the girl food. Delivering the food and seeing her sorry condition, the Indian took pity on her and decided to help her escape. He told her when to be ready, at which time he would loosen her tethers. Near the teepee, close but out of sight, a horse would be waiting. Just before the hour of their escape, the brave rehearsed the leap from ledge to ledge he would have to make. When the appointed hour came, the brave cut the girl's ties. They made it to the horse unseen, but as they rode off, a sentry spotted them and put up the alarm, rousing the whole camp. Followed closely by the other Indians of the tribe, the brave navigated his horse from ledge to ledge, the girl clasped tightly behind him. Again and again he jumped, but his tribe followed. On the final ledge, the Indian narrowly mistimed his jump, and the brave, the girl and the horse fell hundreds of feet to a grisly death below.

THE MASS HOUSE

The Mass House is a popular destination for teenagers in Hanover. The lone house sits on the left side of Mines Road, five hundred yards off the road behind a gated driveway. In the Mass House in the early 1940s, a young man killed his wife, his infant daughter and then himself. Traveling to the house at night, the infant's terrified cries still ring through the air. Legend trippers park on the road and walk to the house hoping to hear the baby's wail. Others report seeing the ghost of the mother holding her child in the upstairs window.

OLD CENTER STREET MANSION

Young schoolgirls leaving Millersburg's local movie theater and heading to Nelson's ice cream parlor had to pass the Old Center Street Mansion, host to a legend of a tragic death and a ghostly red hand. An eccentric gentleman built the house many years ago. The peculiar man's best friend was his pet monkey. When the monkey died, the man gave him a full funeral and buried him beneath an elegant gravestone near his back door. The weathered brick home had numerous stairwells and halls and purportedly was full of secret passageways. The small window on the side of the house, behind a shrub- and weed-covered walkway, was of particular interest to the girls.

As the young girls hurried past the house as fast as their little legs could carry them, they would see something signaling them from this window. The community knew that strange things had happened in the house years ago, the worst of which involved a young maid who worked for the old man. She had fallen in love with a handsome young deliveryman and wished to leave the old man's service. When she told the old man her wishes, he refused. When she insisted, he imprisoned her, and she died in the house. The young maid is now condemned for all time to wave to other young girls passing by, begging them to help her escape. Now, when it's dark and young girls linger too long staring at the window, the shape of a hand forms in the dark mist of a red, bloodlike shadow. A cosmetologist purchased the mansion, ironically hoping to turn it into a popular shop for young girls. The business failed, and the house now stands empty once again, except for the monkey, which still keeps vigil at the back door.

PETER ALLEN HOUSE

During the mid-eighteenth century, William Penn's grandson, John Penn, was a bit of a rogue. Driving his father crazy as usual, he ran off and married a Scotch-Irish girl. His good English Quaker father had forbidden the marriage, but love triumphed, and the two married secretly in England. Like anyone who traveled in South Central Pennsylvania, John Penn knew the frontier innkeeper Peter Allen, who owned the place where one stayed when crossing the Susquehanna. Because the Penns promised to break up the marriage, John enlisted Peter to help keep the couple safe. Peter agreed, and John and his wife lived happily for a while, but the wealthy Penns enlisted Indians to kidnap John's wife and haul her to Canada.

The loss devastated John at first, but soon enough he found a new wife. Many years later, stopping once again at the Peter Allen House, John ran into a sickly woman on the verge of death. She told a story of Indians dragging her to Canada. She escaped and was trying to return to her beloved husband. John Penn suddenly recognized his first wife, who died in his arms.

In a second legend, set in the early twentieth century, the Peter Allen House played host to a wedding. The bride finished preparing for her big day. Ready to make the plunge, she began walking from the bridal room to the ceremony grounds. As she was walking, an oncoming carriage ran her over, killing her. Her ghost haunts the Peter Allen House to this day.

REHMEYER'S HOLLOW

In 1928, John Blymire experienced a streak of bad luck. Convinced that someone in the community had placed a hex on him, he turned to the local witches of the area for help. Desperate to remove the curse, he approached Clara Horner. Unable to remove the curse, she recommended he try the River Witch, Nellie Noll of Lancaster County. Nellie Noll informed John that Nelson Rehmeyer had placed a hex on him. Blymire was familiar with the witch Nelson Rehmeyer, who had once used his powwow powers to cure Blymire as a child. Although hesitant to accept this at first, Noll removed a dollar bill from Blymire's hand, causing Rehmeyer's face to appear. Now sufficiently convinced, he heeded instruction from the River Witch. Noll told Blymire that to remove the hex he must complete one of two tasks. The first option was to steal a lock of Rehmeyer's hair and bury it in the earth between six and eight feet. The second was to nab Rehmeyer's copy of the powwow grimoire *The Long Lost Friend* and burn it.

Now firm in his resolve to take action against his one-time healer, Blymire decided to enlist help. He found John Curry, a troubled seventeen-year-old, and Wilbert Hess, a fourteen-year-old whose family had fallen on hard times. To instill the proper commitment in his co-conspirators, he convinced them that Nelson Rehmeyer had hexed them too. Traveling to Rehmeyer's home, the crew spent the first night enjoying Rehmeyer's hospitality. After food and conversation, he invited the three men to spend the night in his home. Blymire felt that Rehmeyer knew their true purpose and was acting with such hospitality to toy with them.

On the second night, Rehmeyer showed no such hospitality. He denied knowledge of any powwow book, and a scuffle broke out between the men. Rehmeyer was tied, beaten and burned. Blymire was arrested for murder the following day. Feeling that he had done the right thing, Blymire gave a full confession, including his motive for the killing. Already feeling the weight of the hex lifted, Blymire exclaimed, "Thank God! The witch is dead." Although neither the book nor lock of hair was taken from Rehmeyer's home, the three did pilfer ninety-seven cents, adding a burglary charge to the murder case.

The three had a speedy trial, one in which little was heard about powwow, hexes or witchcraft. Prosecutors said that the missing ninety-seven cents suggested a motive of burglary rather than witchcraft. The national spotlight focused on an old custom embarrassed county residents. Powwow was little-known outside the Pennsylvania Dutch region, and the tremendous attention forced powwow underground and prompted the creation of the Pennsylvania Medical Practices Act. By 1928, Blymire and Curry had received life in prison, and a judge sentenced Hess to ten to twenty years.

Blymire served twenty-four years of his life sentence and was paroled. Curry was released in 1939 and enlisted in the armed forces in 1943, serving in World War II. Upon his return from the war, Curry lived out his years as a farmer and an artist, a skill he had picked up in prison.

Since November 28, 1928, there has been constant interest in Rehmeyer's Hollow. The murder forms part of the intrigue, but the legend of that tragic day has taken on a life of its own and shaped new narratives. Today, Rehmeyer's Hollow, a heavily wooded and eerie place where the sun never seems to shine, hosts not just legend trips but also parties, séances and additional haunted happenings. Although Rehmeyer was beaten to death and then burned, visitors report seeing his ghost hanging from a tree or on his porch. A boy, likely Rehmeyer's son, has reportedly been seen peeking out of Rehmeyer's window, and vehicles are

Many Months Before York Lives Down Its "Spook" Reputation

It will be many months before York lives down the reputation, gained for it by the Rehmyer murder and its exploitation by metropolitan newspapers, of being a backwoods community where men ride in 1912 Fords and women, wrinkled and snaggle-toothed, use brooms as a means of transportation.

If travelers returning home from distant cities are to be believed, people who never heard of Salem know all about York and the Rehmyer witchcraft murder. Scarcely a newspaper in the country has neglected the "witchcraft" killing, or failed to recognize it as a sensation, and the mere mention of their own home town, Yorkers say, starts a discussion of witches and "spooks." Each discussion makes necessary the performance of the patriotic duty on the part of Yorkers of trying to convince a doubtful audience that York is no more "spooky" than any other American city.

Right: Vintage 1928 newspaper clipping bemoaning the stain that Nelson Rehmeyer's murder will put on the national reputation of York County. *Courtesy of the Archives of Pennsylvania Folklife and Ethnography.*

Below: Nelson Rehmeyer's house in Rehmeyer's Hollow in 1989. *Courtesy of the Archives of Pennsylvania Folklife and Ethnography.*

likely to stall while passing by the house. In addition to the now haunted house, a door to hell supposedly waits in the vicinity of Rehmeyer's long-since-razed barn—a door that has never been found. In addition to the house and the barn, the hollow has a haunted bridge as well. Particularly popular among teenagers, the legend trippers park their cars on the bridge, kill the ignition and wait. As the spooked driver turns the key in the ignition, he finds that the engine will not start.

In addition to the haunted house where the crime took place, the Sadler Church Cemetery, Rehmeyer's final resting place a few miles away from his home, is also allegedly haunted. Unlike Rehmeyer's house—now the private property of a grouchy owner—Rehmeyer's grave is open to the general public, although people are supposed to visit during daylight hours. Regardless, Rehmeyer's tombstone receives frequent visitors during the witching hour. Those who conduct séances in the cemetery report feeling Rehmeyer's spirit, one that is particularly willing to respond to calls for signs of his presence.

Commercial enterprise has also taken advantage of the popularity of Rehmeyer's Hollow. The Winterstown Fire Company offered a popular Halloween hayride in the hollow for many years that included screams, voices and (blank) shots fired. The annual hayride has since been disbanded because of noise complaints from locals. While ending a practice that was no doubt cacophonous each October, the neighborhood may have made a mistake. What once was a safe and regulated approach to satisfying the legend tripping urge once a year has now, by necessity, been replaced by individual, spontaneous trips to the hollow.

It's difficult to determine whether the popularity of the legend trip is due to the grisly murder, Rehmeyer's status as a confirmed witch or, most likely, a combination of the two. The legend seems to lack clear-cut villains and victims. Rehmeyer was murdered, but history has been kind to his killers and not completely sympathetic to him. The belief in hexes ran deep in South Central Pennsylvania, and the idea that Rehmeyer had indeed hexed Blymire seemed plausible to those who kept the legend alive. At the time of the events described, powwow was a major source of embarrassment for York County.

In a survey of 110 York County teenagers administered in 1989 by Susan Lynn Schiding, 96 percent said that they had heard of Rehmeyer's Hollow; 76 percent of them knew the exact location of the Hollow; and of those who knew where to find Rehmeyer's Hollow, 80 percent of them had been there at least one time. Over half of the respondents had heard the legend from other friends, but parents had initiated a surprising 25 percent. The majority had heard the legend before they turned twelve, and 25 percent had heard it before they turned ten. When asked why the hollow is famous, only 22 percent knew the history of Nelson Rehmeyer and John Blymire. Most teenagers gave alternate responses. Following is just a sampling of the more interesting responses.

- *The green house in the hollow is haunted. The Hex is all about the hollow. The house has a treasure in it and Rehmeyer's ghost guards it.*
- *The story of Ichabod Crane, and the headless horseman.*
- *A kid killed his parents.*
- *The homeowners will murder anyone who tries to go in the house.*
- *An old man with a gun shoots trespassers.*
- *Ouija boards work best there.*
- *Somebody was burned by a devil worshiper.*
- *The house burned but no bodies were ever found.*
- *People who go there are killed and buried under the floor of the house.*
- *A headless witch rides a horse around the hollow.*
- *A couple parked their car there, and a man came after them with a knife.*
- *If you go through on Halloween night, Rehmeyer will come after you. His ghost still haunts people today.*
- *Go there, and you'll never come out!*
- *Rehmeyer's ghost will possibly grab you on Halloween and take you with him driving through the hollow.*
- *Rehmeyer's car drives around by itself on full moons.*
- *The gateway to hell is there. If you go through the seven gates of hell, one year later you will die.*
- *To get rid of Rehmeyer's spirit, you have to walk around your car three times.*

- *If you go past three times in a car and shut off your car the third time, you can't get it started again.*
- *The wallpaper bleeds.*
- *The walls cannot be painted. If you try, they just start to bleed.*
- *A rock bleeds and objects float around without explanation.*
- *There is a red-eyed deer there.*
- *Some girl was killed when her boyfriend left to go get gas for the car.*
- *People say that blood drips from his grave at midnight on Halloween.*
- *The Ku Klux Klan has their hideout there, and they burn crosses and black people there.*
- *A man was hacked to death by an axe and his ghost is still around cutting the heads off of passing tourists.*
- *At Halloween if you get caught by him there you'll die from him murdering you with an axe.*
- *In the early 1900s, there lived a witch in the Red Lion Area at a place called Rehmeyer's Hollow. Well, at least this man called his wife a witch. There were a lot of killings going on at the time and he claimed it was her work. No one believed him so he killed her himself and was then put on trial for her murder. The trial came up finding him guilty of murder. Meanwhile in jail he died of unnatural causes. It was believed that she came back and killed him. Not long after the trial some reporters wanted to take pictures of the place where Rehmeyer lived, so they did. When they got the pictures back there were none. None of the pictures turned out; every one was blank. To this day you can't go on this property without something weird happening.*
- *There's a farmhouse in Rehmeyer's Hollow. Some neighbors said that one day the cows were mooing and making a lot of racket. This went on for days. There was a large family living in the house. People went down to investigate and all the children were lying dead, face down on the grass outside, and the parents were missing. All the later owners still felt the presence of these former people. They heard children crying and cows mooing although there are no longer any cows or children. The house is now abandoned.*
- *I hear tell a witch was murdered there and his head was chopped off. So now his ghost roams the Hollow looking for victims. I forget*

what really happened there, but that's the story my friends told me when I was younger.

- *This murdered witch Rehmeyer is supposed to haunt the Hollow, but I don't know anyone who's seen him. I've heard two rumors about that place: 1) that the blood on the walls and floors cannot be covered by wallpaper and carpet; 2) on a full moon night you can see a man running without a head being chased by his murderers. I think one is still in jail.*
- *I've been to the Hollow partying often and one time when we were in a pick-up truck we heard dogs far off. All of a sudden we were surrounded by ten or fifteen dogs who wouldn't let us leave. Then as quickly as they had arrived, they vanished. One of the guys I was with said they were the ghost dogs that guard Rehmeyer's property for their murdered master.*
- *One thing is for certain; Rehmeyer's Hollow is one place you do not want to go if you have a weak heart. The place appears to*

Nelson Rehmeyer's gravestone in the cemetery at Sadler's Church in Stewartstown. *Courtesy of the Archives of Pennsylvania Folklife and Ethnography.*

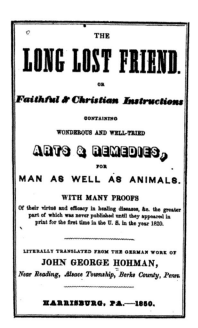

The cover of the powwow holy text *The Long Lost Friend*. This is the book John Blymire went to Rehmeyer's Hollow to find. *Courtesy of Harvard College Library.*

be haunted and smells like it also. Even today at Halloween, the witches and warlocks of York County come together at midnight in the hollow and perform their rites and rituals.

- When you go legend tripping in the hollow there is a house which is believed to be old man Rehmeyer's. Supposedly he still haunts the house on occasion. No one would dare to go inside because you won't be able to leave. The property is very run down and shamble-like. Old legend has it that if you proceed down the hollow while in a vehicle past dusk and the light from inside the house goes on—you will NOT make it out of the hollow alive. You may proceed at no risk at daylight hours. If you walk the two mile stretch at night, it is a given that you are flirting with the devil himself, not to mention Rehmeyer's companionship.

- People actually went up to the house, touched it, and ran back to their car. They proceeded to try and get their car started and it would not start. Then a small light would appear on the side of the house. And then and only then would the car finally turn over. They go safely home, and swear that they will never go down to the hollow ever again.

- *People I grew up with say that if you want and swear that you are going to go inside the house, as you get there a force overcomes you at the front door. You cannot overcome it and you change your mind.*
- *This tale was told to me by a classmate who hunts in the hollow in the fall. His grandfather told him the story. Old man Rehmeyer had a relationship with a Ms. Gibson. Ms. Gibson was a fairly attractive woman in her twenties. Well, Rehmeyer took a liking to her and she to him. Some say that Nelson used his powers to make her weak to everyone else but him. Ms. Gibson found Rehmeyer a gentle but mysterious man with a lot of character. John Blymire lived in the next hollow over. To this day the next hollow over from Rehmeyer's is Blymire's Hollow. He found out about this relationship. Blymire being around the same age as Ms. Gibson, thought that they would make a better couple. So he proceeded to make advances without any return on her part. At this point Blymire was furious and jealous. He contacted a powwower who had told him that Rehmyer had placed a curse on him. He told him that the only way to take it off was to get a lock of his hair. Well, Blymire was a determined man. When he got to the residence, Rehmeyer was alone and he put up a fight. Blymire had to kill him to get it. After the deed had been done, Blymire went back to the powwower and he told John that he had to get rid of the woman closest to Nelson because she knew of his powers and curses. Blymire and the powwower then found Ms. Gibson the following evening and hanged her from a tree. Later, she was buried next to the tree. Still to this day in the middle of a field in the Hollow stands a tree, the tombstone, and the grim reminder of a what might have happened there.*

Basilica of the Sacred Heart Catholic Church

The Basilica of the Sacred Heart Catholic Church in Hanover is the oldest stone Catholic church in the United Sates. In the late 1800s, the church was but a small chapel. Growth in the congregation required an expansion. The new church extended over a cemetery, which was controversial at the time. According to legend, the new church had a youth choir led by a nun, and the altar had a choir lot with large brass pipes over the organ. Behind the organ, a door led up to the pipes. The nun told the children in the choir that if they ever saw the door moving, they were to turn their heads and flee the church immediately. One day during Mass, the door moved, and the children in the choir ran out of the church. But the nun, ignoring her own advice, looked at the door. From that day forward, she was in a permanent state of shock and had to be sent to an insane asylum. Catholic elementary school students in Hanover, where the church is still active, circulate the legend to this day.

THREE MILE ISLAND

On March 28, 1979, the Three Mile Island Nuclear Power Station was the site of the worst nuclear meltdown in the history of the United States. In a series of investigations in the aftermath of the meltdown, the government refused to admit the possibility of sickness from the spread of nuclear radiation. The official report stated "the level of radiation exposure as calculated for the worst case (at Middletown, 100 mrem) was less than $1/1000^{th}$ of that which might have caused clinically detectable effects." The report concluded that "based on the available data, it appears that none of the reported plant and animal health effects discussed above can be directly attributed to the operation of the accident at the Three Mile Island Nuclear Power Station." Regardless, numerous legends about the deleterious effects of the radiation spread through the area surrounding Three Mile Island.

Birdwatchers detected a noticeable drop in starling and robin populations during the spring and summer of 1979, a point conceded by government authorities. Hunters noticed a drop in squirrels, rabbits, pheasants and other small game, and biologists feared that the hop toad had become completely extinct. Some felt that the radiation was killing plants as well as animals.

Residents reported a variety of species of trees with an unusual amount of dead branches and leaves. One farmer complained that his pear trees were producing less fruit than in previous years, and the plants

The Three Mile Island cooling towers, forming a backdrop for tiny Goldsboro, Pennsylvania, on April 6, 1979, one week after the nuclear meltdown. *Courtesy of the National Archives.*

around a cemetery and a water trough in the area had all died. On May 2, 1979, a Dauphin County housewife submitted an official complaint to the Pennsylvania Bureau of Foods and Chemistry about a glowing fish. She had purchased a shad at the local supermarket and cut it into pieces. Her husband then took it into their dark basement, where he noticed an unsettling glow. Authorities brushed it off as bacteria.

Residents near the Susquehanna River reported seeing a "white powder" floating on the river. Some reported seeing it after rains, some during the growing season and some year round. Authorities claimed that they weren't able to collect any samples but assured residents that it was probably pollen. Biologists worried that the mollusk population might be in danger. A doctoral candidate in biology from the University of Maryland spent several years around Three Mile Island trying to assess the risk to the mollusk population. I asked his family about the results of his research. They are unknown. The researcher succumbed to leukemia at Johns Hopkins University before he could finish his dissertation.

Toad Road

A big mansion sits off of a dirt road near Druck Valley. Locals call it Toad Road. A big iron gate blocks the long driveway back to the mansion, but the gate is usually open. People who have been back there say that about one-eighth of a mile down the driveway, the first of several signs appears. The first reads, "Enter at Your Own Risk." Continuing down the lane, the signs get harsher. The most legendary of the signs features a poem warning anyone proceeding past that point that they will be turned into a toad. Reaching the poem sign, the mansion is clearly visible in the foreground. Dogs bark in the distance, and another sign promises that the owners will release the dogs on unwelcome guests. The owner of the house is supposedly an evil doctor, linked to the devil worshipers of Druck Valley. One female legend tripper reported meeting a white Cadillac near the house. Every time the Cadillac passed another car on the road, the other car stalled, including her own car. Restarting her car, she and her friends attempted to follow the Cadillac, but it vanished into thin air.

Gravity Hill

A hundred miles southwest of Harrisburg in Bedford County sits a hill. In some ways, it is a hill like any other. A road runs up the middle; thick greenery flanks either side. But this is not any ordinary hill. This is "Gravity Hill." The forces of nature work differently here. Teenagers of driving age have made legend trips to Gravity Hill and its many national variants for decades. For example, I collected the following verbatim text about York County's Gravity Hill:

I was in college—and a bunch of friends and I decided to go do something super spooky for the night, something we heard from some sleazy guy at the bar. I do believe he was attempting to get some action but we ditched him and went by ourselves. He gave us a napkin with directions written on it. My friend Katie drove us and we found it pretty *easily. No other cars were there. It's up past the Dover area. We turned near Pinchot Park and took a right and headed over some train tracks. I think near the ski place? I can't remember any road names; probably due to the extracurricular activities at the time of the adventure. We were high out of our minds, talking about the legend on the way and how afraid we were! We pulled up to the road and were surprised how on your right there is basically a cliff right there, so we kinda believed the "story" even more. We drove up the hill, did a U-turn and then went down to right before the stop sign. We put the car in neutral and Katie took her foot off the pedals…*dun dun dun…*And the car very slowly did in fact go up the hill! As though we were being pushed by a bus full of high school football players as the story was told to us by the patron at the bar. We did it a few times and each time the car was "pushed" up the hill. Good times, good times.*

Searching "Gravity Hill" on any search engine brings up gravityhill.com as one of the first two hits. The website's only real competitor is the "Gravity Hill" entry on Wikipedia. Although there are hundreds of Gravity Hills around the world, gravityhill.com pertains specifically to the Gravity Hill located in New Paris, Bedford County, Pennsylvania. Here the legend seeker finds a polished and playful site that *encourages* interested parties to try out Gravity Hill.

The first thing that stands out on the homepage is the Gravity Hill traffic sign. The theme colors of the page are otherwise gray and brown, but the traffic sign is bright yellow. It is of the "warning sign" type, but instead of warning of pedestrians, equestrians or cyclists, it warns of Gravity Hill. Both the "G" and the "Y" are made of arrows, commenting on gravity's capriciousness in this zone. Unlike most warning signs, however, this sign calls out to motorists, daring them to visit the hill. Below the sign are three fast-changing images of Gravity Hill. All three are intriguing, and none is completely satisfying. The image changes every three seconds. Once every six seconds, the viewer finds himself looking at the starting point of the Gravity Hill. On the ground, painted in white spray paint, are the words "START" and "GH." Once every twelve seconds, one of two other images appear. The first is a blue exercise ball set on the starting mark. The other is a second Gravity Hill sign. This one does not warn but rather simply points to the location of Gravity Hill. It is located directly beneath the street signs for Bethel Hollow Road and Cortland Road, a concession to the "folk." On Bedford's Gravity Hill, the official and the unofficial seem to collide in usual ways. The location is both the corner of Bethel Hollow and Cortland and Gravity Hill.

Gravity Hill has a typical, sad narrative, but that is left out of the website's narrative. It prefers to focus on the antigravity aspect—the Bermuda Triangle of South Central Pennsylvania—rather than risk creating fear and bad feelings through discussing the tragic, untimely death of children (the usual explanation for Gravity Hill's antigravity properties):

> *Have you ever wanted to defy gravity? You could book a seat on the space shuttle, but by the time you buy a ticket, rent your space suit and drive to the launch site, you'll have well over $10 invested. For a lot less (free actually), you can defy gravity in Bedford County, PA. Located in the suburbs of New Paris, PA (South Central Pennsylvania)… Gravity Hill is a phenomenon. Cars roll uphill and water flows the wrong way. It's a place where gravity has gone haywire. There is no fee to venture onto Gravity Hill. It is quite simply a road in a remote corner of Bedford County. Call us at (800) 765-3331 to receive a free copy of the Gravity Hill brochure…or, for inspiration, testimony, directions and more, click away, gallant soul.*

Also notable are the "Top 10 Reasons to Visit Gravity Hill," a reference to *The Late Show with David Letterman*, *The Dick Clark Show*, *People* magazine and others with well-known top ten lists. (The site concedes that there are probably over a million, but it could only think of ten.) Like these other lists, Gravity Hill's list descends from ten to one. Although they are lighthearted, each is significant. The first is a call to skeptics: "10. If your glass is half empty, your outlook can only improve." A legend, by definition, leaves room for skepticism. The website uses the first of its list to address these worries, promising doubters that there is literally nothing to lose by journeying to Gravity Hill. In the worst-case scenario, they will feel the same as they did in the beginning. The next two are rather lame jokes about gravity: "9. Ice cream cones aren't as messy on a hot day," and, "8. Less chance of birds splattering your clean car." The rest are more intriguing. Although still playful, they touch, perhaps unconsciously, on themes common to legend tripping: "7. The wonder bra works better than advertised," "6. Light beer… even lighter," "5. Last place the cops would think to look for you," "4. It's free…but you can impress everyone with tales of booking the place for a cool 'C' note," "3. Less chance of life-threatening injury ingesting pop-rocks," "2. Less overflow from those saggy diapers that leak" and finally, "1. It's not the end of the world…but you can see it from here."

Perhaps even more intriguing, the website presents a faux-informant. Listed as an "eyewitness," Dennis Murphy is not just anyone; he's a man of the cloth. Dennis Murphy grew up as a "97 pound weakling, afraid of his own shadow." He underwent a life-changing transformation one summer afternoon after experiencing the power of Gravity Hill. He decided to become a Bedford County hermit, devoting his life to meditation on the event. According to Friar Murphy, "After living through that shocking experience of an earth with no gravity, I came to understand that everything else in life is small potatoes. It helped me put the rest of my fears in perspective. I then decided to devote my life to meditation about that experience." The site includes a picture of Friar Murphy. He looks like Neil Patrick Harris in a friar's robe. According to the website, beginning February 13, 2003, the Vatican directed Friar Murphy to cease all interviews concerning Gravity Hill.

One of the prime indicators of any piece of folklore is in-group knowledge. One knows how to perform a custom because he has learned it informally over time. The Gravity Hill website, on the other hand, includes a Gravity Hill etiquette section, putting in print how to properly behave on the hill: "1. Check your rearview mirror before doing the hill backwards," "2. Never turn around in the locals' yards," "3. Wave and smile when folks pass by," "4. Let folks by if they're trying to get past you" and finally, "5. Be Courteous. Some families live out beyond this road." Folklore attempts to control behavior by establishing norms. Government does so through ordinances, and businesses use rules. The classification of Gravity Hill (like the classification of a Visitor's Bureau) is ambiguous. At Bedford's Gravity Hill, there are none of the safeguards often found in twentieth-century America. The site attempts to create customary etiquette that will provide security in an otherwise unstructured environment.

One section of the website falls prey to classic legend commodification: gifts. On this page, consumers can mark their adventure through the purchase of clichéd tourist items: T-shirts, bumper stickers, magnets, car decals and coffee mugs. The items are not inexpensive—the coffee mug alone is twenty dollars. Merchandise is available to all—small, medium, large and extra large, as well as in colors ranging from black to pink. Perhaps the most unsettling aspect is the supposed ability to take an indescribable feeling like that felt at Gravity Hill and "add it to a cart" (shipping and handling included in price). All items, the page assures us, are also available for sale in the Bedford County Visitors Center.

Gravity Hill is also included as part of the "Covered Bridge Driving Tour" section. In fact, it is the exact midpoint of the tour. This page mentions that "you need to decide if you want to visit the often talked about, but seldom found, Gravity Hill." Unlike on Gravity Hill's page, on the Covered Bridge Driving Tour's page it seems almost like an interruption, a non sequitur on an otherwise quaint self-guided covered bridge tour. The tourist—who to this point has been treated to a nostalgic trip past four nineteenth-century wooden structures, each with its own name and construction date (e.g., Claycomb, Snook's and Dr. Kniseley's)—is suddenly asked to "look for the letters 'GH' spray painted on the road" and "a telephone pole with the number 69." In an otherwise polished and linear tour, Gravity Hill offers a blip on the radar. The Bedford County Visitors Center, it seems, almost revels in the juxtaposition of folkloric destinations.

Bedford's Gravity Hill was featured on PBS's *Dave and Dave*, about two men who travel around having "excellent adventures." They decided to explore Gravity Hill as part of their "Strange PA" show. "To those of you who may have never heard of this…it's either an optical illusion or some sinister step into a bizarre world where up is seemingly down and vice versa!" When they tried Gravity Hill in a minivan, the vehicle "appear[ed] to drift up hill." But they attempted the same experiment with an exercise ball, and the ball just rolled off the road.

Bedford County is relying on Gravity Hill as a prime tourist attraction. Although the powers that be find it necessary to reduce their solemnity when promoting such a venue, easily seen in the comparison from one Bedford County site to the other, this is nonetheless a top tourism site in Bedford County, according to Bedford County natives. The unanimous opinion I received when questioning residents was that there are very few others draws in Bedford County. In an already rural South Central Pennsylvania, Bedford County is one of the most rural spots. Nonetheless, business infrastructure exists, one that is willing to put money into "tourism" if it means annual profit. If this means promoting Gravity Hill, then Gravity Hill it will be. Folklore has long held touristic value, from Abraham Lincoln's apocryphal log cabin birthplace to women's quilts, but a legend trip as a sponsored tourist site seems to be a new idea.

MEMORIAL AUDITORIUM

The Masquers and SSC Music Theatre is a theater organization on Shippensburg University's campus. Ann, a fifteen-year member of the Masquers, is the oldest person around who knows the ghost stories of Memorial Auditorium, although the ghost (or ghosts) has haunted the theater since long before even Ann joined. The place has always been haunted, but the hauntings felt tamer when she began. Originally, the stories focused on the staircase on the stage left of the auditorium. Walking down the steps, the fifth step from the bottom would vanish. And those who did reach the bottom reported a chilly feeling that told them they weren't supposed to be down there. A man killed in the steam pipe recess is supposedly the reason for the haunting. The happenings were scary enough that, despite ample space, nothing was stored on that side of the Memorial Auditorium at all. Stories circulated that something wasn't quite right in the attic either, but the major haunting at the time was the staircase.

It wasn't until later that the truly creepy hauntings began. A crew of five or six costumers often worked until two, three or four o'clock in the morning. Between two and three o'clock in the morning, they would report hearing steps in the hallway, even though they were the only people in the building. They would see something white walk past the door, but when they peeked their heads out, it would be gone. Sometimes they would hear it walk up and down the stairs.

Walking into the attic, they were overwhelmed with the feeling that they were being intensely watched by something malevolent. Even with the lights on, the Masquers report the same feeling. This is especially strange because the auditorium is not a new or unknown space. Several members have been there for as many as fifteen years and consider the Memorial Auditorium to be a second home, yet they still get the same feeling. There are nights when the feelings of fear, hostility and coldness are so overwhelming that they just need to leave.

Junior Elena has also had a number of strange experiences in Memorial Auditorium, long before she had heard any of the ghost stories. She was walking down the stage left steps after everybody had left the building, holding onto the railing. Almost at the bottom, she fell, not forward but rather straight down, as if a step had vanished beneath her, even though she was holding onto the handrail and walking carefully one step at a time. She hadn't heard of the haunting and didn't want to spread the word of her clumsiness, so she kept it to herself until she began to hear the other stories.

She also reported sitting backstage with all the doors shut, working on this or that, when suddenly a cold gust of wind blasted through the auditorium. Before these experiences, she was willing to sit in the costume shop alone, but another incident put an end to any solo work. Assigned to sew snap after snap on a burlap costume, she sat alone in the costume shop, working away. Out of the corner of her eye, she kept seeing someone walk past the shop checking on her, but no one else was in the building.

Sophomore Bill was alone in the attic and was one of the last to leave the building that day when a sudden wave of queasiness came over him, a feeling like he had never had before—something that told him he shouldn't be up there and that something horrible was about to happen. He tried to ignore it, but the feeling only got more intense. He checked around but found nothing. Wanting desperately to leave but having too much work to do, he carried on. He hadn't heard of the ghost at that time, and he didn't believe in ghosts anyway. It was only since hearing the other members' ghost stories that he understood what he had experienced.

Two friends told him about the time they had been working late at night in the costume shop with the door closed when in the gap beneath the door one of them saw a shadow walk by. They called out to see who was there but received no response. They were supposed to have been the only ones in the building, and they hadn't heard any of the loud auditorium doors open. They left the costume shop to investigate, but they found no one and heard no one leave. They shook it off as exhaustion and went back to work. But a short while later, a figured walked by again—this time both girls saw it. They jumped up and ran to the door, but again the hallway was empty.

Another ghost sighting happened around Christmas—this one, strangely enough, during the day. Looking at the building while walking through the parking lot, Ann saw the figure of a woman in the costume shop. As it had been her responsibility to lock the doors, Ann knew for a fact that the building was empty. She rechecked every door, and they were indeed all locked. This led to speculation that more than one specter haunted the Memorial Auditorium, since the other ghost was supposedly a man.

The Masquers were rehearsing *Anything Goes*, and sophomore pianist Bryan decided to stay late and practice the titular song, which had to be ready for performance in the Ceddia Union Building (CUB) the next day. He was in the pit with all the lights on playing the song over and over again when the house lights dimmed at about 2:30 a.m. He attributed it to fatigue and continued playing the song. As he was halfway down the page, he felt a hand reach over him, grab the page and tear it from his notebook. He snatched up his notebook and the torn sheet and ran backstage, where he found the dial for every light turned halfway down, even though he was the only one in the auditorium. Suddenly deciding that he had practiced just about enough for one night, he ran out of the auditorium. He assumed that the ghost was sick of hearing the same song over and over again.

Senior Glenda remembered that while student teaching, she would use the typewriter in the Memorial Auditorium office and then run copies off on the ditto machine so she wouldn't have to wake up early and run them off at school. Working past midnight one night, she was left alone in the auditorium. All of the doors were locked, and all Glenda had to do was shut the door behind her when she left. She had finished her exam for the next day and started running it off when she heard footsteps fall from one end of the hall to the other, but no one ever passed the door. Confused but with her mind elsewhere, she continued to run off her exams. Again she heard footsteps padding across the hall, but no one walked by. A bit startled this time, she walked to the hallway to investigate. It was empty. Glenda called out, but received no reply. She convinced herself that it was the night janitor and went back to making her copies. She soon heard the footsteps again, and this time she was sure they had stopped outside the greenroom. Running out to check the hallway, she again found no one.

Starting to become truly upset, she decided to search the entire building. She checked all of the rooms, the restrooms, the stage and the lobby. Everything was still, quiet and dark. As she walked into the greenroom, a chill shot down her spine. The room was ice cold. Glenda grabbed her coat and fled, the copying left unfinished. She turned the light in the office off and pulled the locked door shut, as she had promised. She then had two choices: she could make her way to the light switch, an indirect path that would mean spending more time in the building, or she could take the direct route, which would mean walking out in the dark. She decided to get out as quickly as possible, accepting a short, cringe-inducing walk through the dark auditorium. As Glenda made a beeline for the exit, something scurried behind her all the way to the door. The incident was so vivid in Glenda's mind that she has refused to be alone or the last one in the Memorial Auditorium ever again.

Although many Masquers know generally that a man died in the auditorium years ago, staff technician and fifteen-year member Doug knows the whole story. Way back when the building was under construction and they were plastering the ceilings and the walls, they had scaffolding along the stage right side of the auditorium. A man was climbing up the inside of the scaffolding toward the inside of the house. When the scaffolding fell, the men on top fell over and were only injured, but the man who had been climbing was crushed to death.

Working in the attic, Doug has heard noises that just don't seem right. He tries to wave them off as the air conditioning turning on, but when he checks the air conditioning, it's still off. He'll go back to work and hear the same noise again, but another search finds nothing. Sooner or later, Doug usually comes to the conclusion that he's tired and that the night's task would be even better tomorrow in the daylight with a few helpers nearby.

Staff technician Chris was similarly spooked. Doug came in one night to find Chris sitting in the middle of the auditorium with every light in the house turned on.

"What are you sitting in the middle of the auditorium for? Aren't you supposed to be fixing lights?" Doug asked.

"I was fixing lights," Chris replied.

"Why aren't you fixing the lights now?"

"I was waiting for you."

"You couldn't fix them until I got here?"

"Nope."

"Why not?"

"I don't like it in the attic."

"What do you mean you don't like it in the attic?"

"I don't like it in the attic. This building breathes."

"What do you mean this building breathes?" And then Doug added, "You mean the ventilation? The air conditioning?"

"Nope."

"Well, what do you mean?"

"I mean something's not right about this building."

Doug dragged Chris back up to the attic. "I don't hear anything, Chris."

"You can usually only hear it when you're alone," Chris replied.

But as they finished up for the night and began walking out of the attic, they heard the building take a breath. They methodically worked their way through the entire building, checking every nook and cranny, theater sidearms (mounting lights) in hand. Their search that night came up empty yet again. During *Equus*, while up on the catwalk checking the lights alone and in the dark, Doug heard the breathing again. He doesn't work alone in attic anymore.

Although the ghosts have been there for decades, the increased intensity of the haunting may be the fault of the costume shop, whose members admitted to bringing in Ouija boards and riling up the spirits. Ever since, Masquers agree that the Memorial Auditorium has been filled with the cold, unease, dread and hostility of a lingering presence.

FURTHER READING

Those interested in further reading on South Central Pennsylvania folklore should look first to the Archive of Pennsylvania Folklife and Ethnography at Penn State Harrisburg. The majority of my material came from that one source, although I was only able to cover a small portion of the archive's vast holdings. The archive consists of the Mac Barrick Collection and the Simon Bronner Collection, each holding folklore collected by generations of students at Shippensburg University and Penn State Harrisburg. The archive is open to the general public.

If you are looking for a print source, there is no better series on the subject than *Pennsylvania Folklife*. Run for decades by the Pennsylvania German Society and edited by Don Yoder, the journal is a compendium of Pennsylvania legend and lore. Speaking of Don Yoder, he has been studying Pennsylvania folklore since my parents were in grade school, and I consulted much of his work while putting together this book. I found particularly helpful his essay "The Saint's Legend in the Pennsylvania German Folk Culture" from *American Folk Legend: A Symposium*, an intriguing work that includes Mountain Mary; "Sauerkraut for New Year's" in *The Word & I*, vol. 4; and *Hex Signs: Pennsylvania Dutch Barn Symbols & Their Meaning*. On the subject of hex signs, in addition to Yoder's work, I found David Fooks's "The History of Pennsylvania Barn Stars and Hex Signs," published in *Material Culture*, to be particularly enlightening.

Although a controversial figure, Pennsylvania's first state folklorist cannot be ignored when discussing Pennsylvania folklore. For this work alone I consulted Alfred Shoemaker's *The Pennsylvania Barn, Christmas in Pennsylvania, Eastertide in Pennsylvania, Hex No!, Susquehanna Legends* and *Juniata Memories*. If you like Shoemaker's work, this is but the tip of the iceberg.

Folklore is much older than the idea of folklore collecting, so it is important to look to older sources to mine folkloric data. For the chapter on Pennsylvania Dutch superstitions, I extracted Julius F. Sachse's "Prognostics and Superstitions" from *Pennsylvania-German: A Popular Magazine of Biography, History, Genealogy, Folklore, Literature Etc.*, vol. 3. Davy Crockett's story of the "tam harricoon" came from *Sketches and Eccentricities of Col. David Crockett* by Silas Wright. The legend of the Devil's Hole is found in the *History of Perry County in Pennsylvania from the Earliest Settlement to the Present Time*. There are pamphlets about both William and Elizabeth Wilson: *The Pennsylvania Hermit* and *A Faithful Narrative of Elizabeth Wilson*. "Ghosts of Swatara" is found in *Notes and Queries, Historical and Genealogical, Chiefly Relating to Interior Pennsylvania*, vol. 2. "The Barber's Ghost" is from the 1866 edition of *Baer's Agriculture Almanac*. Mac Barrick wrote an entire essay on the joke in "'The Barber's Ghost': A Legend Becomes a Folktale" in *Pennsylvania Folklife* (Summer 1974).

A number of authors have written monographs on a single legend—or more often the historical background of a legendary subject. One of the best known is Arthur Lewis's *Hex*, a book about the Rehmeyer's Hollow murders. Gary Ludwig did the same for the Blue-Eyed Six in *The Blue-Eyed Six: A Historical Narrative*. Originally intended for publication as a book, Mac Barrick's "Lewis the Robber: A Pennsylvania Folk Hero in Life and Legend" was published posthumously as a monograph in *Midwestern Folklore*, vol. 20. Stanton Friedman's *Crash at Corona* is useful for those interested in UFO legends. On the legend of the Performo Two Company, two books stand out. Torrence Dietz's grandson-in-law, Craig Andrews, wrote *Broken Toy: A Man's Dream, a Company's Mystery*, and Rene Grove's daughter, Grace Grove, wrote *Who Was First: The True Story of the Man Who Really Created Micky*. A recent book related to the Ballad of Susanna Cox is *The*

Hanging of Susanna Cox: The True Story of Pennsylvania's Most Notorious Infanticide and the Legend That's Kept It Alive by Patricia Earnest Suter, Russell Earnest and Corrine Earnest.

Others have approached Pennsylvania legends in shorter chapters and essays. I was delighted when I stumbled across John Weaver's "1967: PA's Capital Becomes the 'UFO Capital,'" both a historical essay and a personal reminiscence. Michael Barton was the first to take seriously "John Harris and the Mulberry Tree" as a story of scholarly interest. His chapter "The Attempted History of John Harris' Burning" can be found in *An Illustrated History of Greater Harrisburg*. David Luthy's chapter on "The Origin and Growth of Amish Tourism" in Donald Kraybill and Marc Olshan's *The Amish Struggle with Modernity* was helpful in deciphering the Amish blue gate legend. Although pertaining to a different Gravity Hill, my favorite Gravity Hill essay is still Carl Lindahl's "Ostensive Healing: Pilgrimage to the San Antonio Ghost Tracks," published in the *Journal of American Folklore*.

INDEX

ABOUT THE AUTHOR

David J. Puglia first became interested in folklore in the fourth grade while studying Greek and Roman mythology. He studied folklore at Western Kentucky University, where he earned a Master of Arts in folk studies. He has worked in the Western Kentucky Folklife Archives, the National Park Service and the Archives of Pennsylvania Folklife and Ethnography. His essay "Getting Maryland's Goat: Origin, Dissemination, and Meaning of Prince George's County's Goatman Legend" won the Buchan Prize for best student essay  from the International Society for Contemporary Legend Research. He is currently a folklorist at Penn State Harrisburg, where he teaches Introduction to American Folklore and American Popular Culture and Folklife. He is pursuing a doctoral degree in American studies. If you would like to contact David, you can reach him at dpuglia@psu.edu.

Visit us at
www.historypress.net